THE DOCTRINE OF THE LAST THINGS

THE DOCTRINE OF THE LAST THINGS;

JEWISH AND CHRISTIAN.

BY

THE REV. W. O. E. OESTERLEY, D.D.

JESUS COLLEGE, CAMBRIDGE.

Wipf and Stock Publishers
199 West 8th Avenue, Suite 3
Eugene, Oregon 97401

The Doctrine of the Last Things
Jewish and Christian
By Oesterley, W.O.E.
ISBN: 1-59244-596-9
Publication date 3/17/2004
Previously published by John Murray, 1908

CONTENTS

PREFATORY NOTE.

For a right understanding of what the Gospels teach concerning the "last things" it is indispensable that the antecedents upon which that teaching was, in the first instance, based should be studied. Eschatology, like so many other things, went through a process of development before it assumed that form which the Gospels have made so familiar to us. No developed growth can be satisfactorily studied without knowing something about its earlier processes of formation and the conditions under which development took place. And, therefore, if we wish to understand what the Gospels teach concerning the "end of the world," the first requisite is that we should have some idea of that earlier teaching upon which it is based. Where is this earlier teaching to be found? Firstly, in the Old Testament; secondly, and chiefly, in the Apocalyptic literature; and thirdly, though in a much less degree, in Rabbinical literature, wherein are re-echoed so many of the popular conceptions on this subject which were current in our Lord's day. It is the main object of the following pages to offer to the general reader some insight into what these three classes of literature have to say upon the subject under consideration.

In order to show in the clearest manner the character of these antecedents, it has been thought well to give a goodly number of quotations from each class of literature. This seemed the more necessary because the connection between the Gospel Eschatology and that which preceded it cannot be adequately realised unless the *ipsissima verba* of each are placed side by side and compared; but it is very tedious to be constantly interrupting the reading by turning up references, and therefore to have these quoted in full before one will, it is hoped, be found to be a considerable convenience. In the case of the Apocalyptic and Rabbinical literatures it seemed doubly necessary to give quotations, and not merely references, because many of the editions of the works belonging to those two classes of literature are, owing to their expense, unavailable for those who have not the use of a good theological library.

But while the purpose of this book is, in the main, to present in popular form an outline of the antecedents of Christ's doctrine of the "last things," it is impossible to remain altogether silent upon some topics which inevitably suggest themselves. When it is found, for example, that there is substantial identity in a number of essential points between the Eschatology of the Gospel and its antecedents, many people will be inclined to wonder whether there is anything at all original and specific in the Gospel teaching on the subject. Therefore it has been attempted here to indicate certain crucial points on which there is a fundamental difference between the Gospel teaching and its antecedents.

Further, another question which arises is as to why it was that Christ based so much of His eschatological teaching, both as regards thought and form, on what had preceded; the attempt is made to answer this question as well.

The whole subject of Eschatology is of vast area; it ramifies to an amazing extent, and it is full of perplexing problems. Of these latter the most critical one is undoubtedly the question as to how far the Eschatology of the Gospels actually represents, on the one hand, the teaching of our Lord, and, on the other, the belief of the early Church. Many people will be inclined to say that this is a preliminary which ought to be dealt with before the subject itself is taken in hand. But the writer has deliberately and of set purpose avoided this thorny subject here, and for several reasons. In the first place, his main object, for the present, has been to examine the antecedents; in the second, the task of attempting to differentiate between the sources of the Gospels is not one to place before general readers; it would necessarily take up a great deal of space, it would involve much diversion from the main subject in hand, and it is quite certain that final conclusions cannot be reached until scholars have expended a great deal more labour upon the problems involved. A third reason is that, in any case, the Gospels are so saturated with Eschatology that even if a great deal of it were eliminated the kernel would remain, and this, as will be seen in the two last chapters of the book, is what really counts.

At the same time the writer is fully aware

that it is only a corner of the subject which is touched upon here; indeed, it is little more than an introduction to one department of the subject that has been attempted.

But, as already hinted, the following pages are not intended for scholars; they are written, in the first place, for the large number of clergy whose manifold parochial duties make it impossible for them to find the requisite time for investigating the subject at first hand themselves, and who, nevertheless, desire to have, in succinct form, an outline of some of the main elements of Eschatology as they existed in pre-Christian times. So that, although very far from exhaustive, the material here offered may, it is hoped, be useful to many of the clergy. In the second place, the writer has had in mind that large and increasing body of lay men and women who are deeply interested in the theological thought of the day, and who may desire to have some insight into one of the various New Testament problems which are exercising the minds of scholars at the present time.

The writer feels it incumbent upon him to take this opportunity of expressing his indebtedness and gratitude to the Rev. Professor Charles for his invaluable editions of Apocalyptic writings; without his published texts and translations, with their suggestive notes, workers in this field of study would be placed at a great disadvantage.

The writer desires also to express his sincere thanks to the Rev. Cyril W. Emmet for his assistance in correcting the proof-sheets.

W. O. E. O.

HATCH END, *Advent* 1908.

THE DOCTRINE OF THE LAST THINGS

CHAPTER I.

THE ANTECEDENTS OF THE GOSPEL TEACHING: INTRODUCTORY.

THE Christian Religion has its roots in, and has grown out of, the Jewish Religion. This is a statement of fact which nobody would be prepared to deny. The Old Testament was written by Jews, mainly about Jews, for Jews; the New Testament was written by Jews,[1] to whom the Old Testament was the "Word of God"; what the "Scriptures," *i.e.*, the Old Testament, said was to them authoritative as nothing else was; and therefore the New Testament, and especially the Gospels, is permeated with Jewish belief and thought. When Christ teaches, He bases His teaching, in the first instance, upon Jewish

[1] The third Gospel and the Acts forming the only exceptions.

doctrine; He develops that doctrine, expands it, spiritualises it, when needful; but His teaching, like that of His Church, is founded upon the teaching of the prophets. *Think not that I came to destroy the Law, or the Prophets: I came not to destroy, but to fulfil. For verily I say unto you, Till heaven and earth pass away, one jot or one tittle shall in no wise pass away from the law, till all things be accomplished.*[1] This principle is further insisted upon in the words: *The scribes and the Pharisees sit in Moses' seat; all things therefore whatsoever they bid you, these do and observe.*[2] This second passage is very pointed, for our Lord testifies to the correctness of Pharisaic teaching, though He goes on to denounce the failure of the Pharisees to carry out their teaching in practice. And it is upon this Pharisaic teaching that, in the first instance, He bases His own. As far as it went, and as far as it was not a perversion, as it was in some cases, of the precepts of the Law (as, *e.g.*, in Matt. xxiii. 23, 24), the teaching of the Pharisees was in accordance with the "teaching of Moses"; and therefore Christ's command to the people to observe whatsoever the Pharisees taught was

[1] Matt. v. 17, 18.

[2] Matt. xxiii. 2, 3.

altogether what might have been expected. The scribes and Pharisees were together the keepers of the Law, and in this respect they were faithful and loyal to their trust; but as students of the Law, as well as keepers and teachers, their guilt was all the greater when hypocrisy and self-seeking contaminated their orthodoxy. Their claim to be better than other men, which the very name "Pharisee" implied ("one who separates himself" from others, and thus attains, or has attained, a higher degree of sanctity), was in itself of the nature of spiritual pride. But in spite of this, it is very necessary to remember that numbers of their body must have been genuine and true men (*cf.*, *e.g.*, John iii. 1ff.), and that they were the real upholders of orthodoxy against such teachers of heresy as the Sadducees. What they taught, therefore, was the teaching of Moses and the prophets; and this was, at any rate, one of the antecedents of the Gospel teaching, and therefore upon it Christ based, in part, His own teaching.

These things are all so obvious that the mention of them may appear superfluous. And yet—what a strange thing it is that Christian theologians, scholars, and teachers so rarely, comparatively speaking, take this obvious fact into consideration. It is well that in our age this is changing, and that more and more it is coming to be seen that the Christian religion can only be adequately understood by studying its beginnings, that early Christian thought and teaching can only be fully grasped when seen in the light of Jewish thought and teaching, that the Gospels can only be fully appreciated when explained from the Jewish point of view, and that the language of the Gospels must be studied in the light of that which the Jews of our Lord's day and of the preceding centuries spoke, whether Aramaic, or a dialect of this, or Hellenistic Greek, and not in the light of that used by classical Greek authors. In a word, there are many signs which point to the fact that the conviction is gaining ground among Christians generally that our religion must be studied and taught and understood from the point of view of its Founder. And since Christ was, according to the flesh, a Jew, brought up according to Jewish ideas (*cf.* Luke ii. 51), and deeply versed in the Jewish Scriptures, uncanonical[1] as well as canonical, we must look to Judaism

[1] For the justification of this statement see below.

—pre-Christian Judaism—as that in which the antecedents of Christian teaching are to be sought.

But in saying that pre-Christian Judaism contained the germs from which Christian teaching was developed, we would guard ourselves from seeming to imply that our Lord in His teaching merely utilised the tenets of Judaism; for this would be as much as to say that there was nothing specifically original or distinctive about Christianity, an assertion to which the contemplation of the Personality of Christ, quite apart from everything else, would give the lie; and clearly the men of our Lord's own day perceived that in His teaching there was something unique and different from that with which they were familiar—*And they were astonished at his teaching: for he taught them as having authority, and not as the scribes*[1]—but while, on the one hand, we see that the teaching of Christ was *sui generis*, that teaching itself tells us, on the other hand, that a very great deal of the content of Christianity constituted the natural development of Judaism. This was necessarily bound to be the case, for Judaism contained a very large amount of

[1] Mark i. 22.

the body of Absolute Truth, the knowledge of which, by divine grace, has been accorded to mankind; and this being so, it could not fail to be embodied in Christian teaching.

Further, in speaking of pre-Christian Judaism, it is indispensable that one should realise that this included two elements which differed greatly from each other, both in their content and in their spirit; they are best expressed under the titles of "Orthodox Judaism" and "Hellenistic Judaism," and both formed the basis of much that Christ taught. It was stated just now that our Lord was deeply versed in uncanonical as well as in canonical Jewish writings, *i.e.*, in Hellenistic Jewish literature as well as in the Old Testament Scriptures. This statement will, it is hoped, be substantiated in chaps. v., vi., vii., below; but here it will be well to indicate as briefly as possible how it came about that, in addition to the Old Testament Scriptures, this new body of Hellenistic Jewish literature came into being.

By the commencement of the second century B.C. Palestinian Judaism had become permeated with Greek thought. This began, in the first instance, through the use of the Greek language, which was, in course of time, the means of the spread of Greek civilisation. It was not only among the Jews of the Dispersion that the influence of the Greek spirit became predominant, that was to be expected; but it was also in Palestine itself that this influence was so strong as to sweep away almost entirely, for a time, all that was best in Judaism. Nothing could be more painfully significant than these words in 1 Macc. i. 11-15: *In those days came there forth out of Israel transgressors of the law, and persuaded many, saying, Let us go and make a covenant with the Gentiles that are round about us; for since we were parted from them many evils have befallen us. And the saying was good in their eyes. And certain of the people were forward herein, and went to the king,*[1] *and he gave them licence to do after the ordinances of the Gentiles. And they built a place of exercise in Jerusalem according to the laws of the Gentiles; and they made themselves uncircumcised, and forsook the holy covenant, and joined themselves to the Gentiles, and sold themselves to do evil.* Such passages are not isolated (*cf.* 2 Macc. ix. 7-17). But while the results of Hellenistic influence were in many respects disastrous among the Jews, in some other respects they were for good. The know-

[1] Antiochus Epiphanes.

ledge of Greek literature and philosophy with which the Jews of the Dispersion came into contact had the effect of breaking down national prejudices and Jewish narrowness; there resulted in these Jews a new mental development, their ideas expanded, their attitude towards men other than those of their own race became more tolerant, a tendency towards Universalism, directly opposed to their traditional Particularism, manifested itself; and the conception which arose in consequence, namely, that of the religion of Jehovah becoming a world religion, and not merely the possession of one people, was a magnificent one, a divinely inspired one, which in due time became realised. The greatest literary products of this blending of Jewish and Greek genius were what is known as the Wisdom literature and the Apocalyptic literature; on this latter see further below, chaps. iv., v.

But as far as Palestinian Judaism was concerned, an altogether new order of things was brought about by the wars of the Maccabees. The nationalist movement which resulted in the Maccabæan victories was utilised by the leading spirits of the nation to crush out, if possible, any lingering remnants of Hellenism; this it failed to do. But it was this nationalist party which was henceforth to hold sway in Palestine; from it came forth the *Pharisees.* Their antagonism to the Hellenistic spirit was wholly justified, both on political and moral grounds; but it must be remembered that at first, at all events, this antagonism arose rather from political than from religious motives. It is most probably the case that ethical purity had much to do with the beginnings of a revolt against Hellenism in Palestine, but it is extremely improbable that this alone would have been effective had it not been for the national question which resulted in the successful Maccabæan wars, because the party which consisted of the faithful adherents of the Law was too small and uninfluential. With the resuscitation of the *national* idea came again particularistic tendencies, and with renewed strength, for there seemed more need than ever for the nation to keep itself from contamination with the Gentiles; the bitterness left behind by the wars went a long way towards widening the breach between Jew and Gentile. And in a natural course there arose now a stricter observance of the Law; this is distinctly observable in official post-Maccabæan literature, and it is reflected in post-Christian Jewish literature, the New Testament writings coming in between the two testifies still further to the fact.

From what has been said it will have been seen that from the rise of the Greek period two parties stood in opposition to each other in Palestine, the orthodox party, and those who demanded and insisted upon greater latitude in belief; the Particularists and the Universalists, the Judaists and the Hellenists. Until the Maccabæan period, the Hellenists were in the ascendant, after that their antagonists held sway; but the two opposing schools of thought each held their own right up to the time when, in the year 70 A.D., the final catastrophe took place, and Jewish national life came to an end. But it is of the first importance to remember that Pharisaism and Hellenism, with all that these two terms imply, played their parts in moulding the religious thought of the Jews long before the Maccabæan period, and continued to do so long after, and that therefore both contributed their *quota* towards the religious development of the people, and in each are to be discovered the antecedents of Gospel teaching.

When it is said, therefore, that Christian teaching must be explained in the light of

Jewish teaching, it will be understood that under "Jewish teaching" are included the two schools of thought referred to above, viz.: Hellenistic Judaism as well as Orthodox Judaism; the latter representing above all things the championship of the Law, the former having as its predominant element eschatological teaching, and being the expression of the thoughts and speculations of the Apocalyptists.

It is almost wholly with the latter that we shall be concerned in the present connection, for upon it was based, to a large extent, the Christian doctrine of the "last things." But the Hellenistic literature, in so far as it deals with Eschatology, is itself based in the first instance upon the teaching of the Old Testament prophets; and therefore, our first duty must be to try and discern in the prophetical writings the leading thoughts which were developed and expanded by the Apocalyptists.

CHAPTER II.

THE ANTECEDENTS OF THE GOSPEL TEACHING: THE OLD TESTAMENT.

IN the prophetical writings of the Old Testament we frequently come across such phrases as "The Day of the Lord," "Those days," "That day," "The last days," etc., and around such expressions[1] there centre certain conceptions and expectations; a brief study of these must be our present task. It is necessary, however, to explain at the outset that it is not with the whole subject of Eschatology in the Old Testament that we propose to deal, but only with those elements which are directly concerned with the purpose in hand, viz.: The antecedents of the Gospel teaching. There are various points in the Eschatological Drama

[1] With the question as to how the ideas which gave birth to these expressions came into being themselves, we are not concerned here; the subject is fully dealt with in the writer's book, *The Evolution of the Messianic Idea* (1908), see especially chaps. x., xi., xvi.

which only indirectly touch our main subject; these we shall leave aside at present, or, at most, merely allude to in passing.

It will be best for the sake of clearness to deal separately, at least as far as this is possible, with those elements which come into consideration here; they are four in number; to these some points of interest, though of subsidiary importance, will be added later on. These four elements in the Old Testament doctrine of the "last things" are as follows:—

i. The Signs which precede the End.
ii. The Advent of Jehovah, the Judge.
iii. The Judgement upon the Wicked.
iv. The Blessedness of the Righteous.

In drawing attention to some of the passages which deal with these, it will clearly be impossible to do so in an exhaustive manner; for, on the one hand, it would become tedious and take up a great deal of space unnecessarily, and, on the other, it would take us too far afield.[1]

[1] It may be thought that the large number of references to be quoted in full in this and the following chapter is unnecessary, and that it would have sufficed to indicate chapter and verse; the reason why the present course has been adopted, is because so many readers find it troublesome to have to be constantly looking up references, and therefore soon give up doing so; but the argument to be considered cannot be adequately followed, unless

§i. *The Signs which precede the End.*

The earliest mention that we have of the "Day of the Lord" is in the book of Amos; for the present we do not enquire as to the reasons why that "Day" was to come about; it is sufficient to say that it heralds the end of things, that it inaugurates a new era,[1] and that certain signs precede the opening of that era. The prophets very frequently connect what they say about this "Day" with the present conditions of the people, or with various historical events; but the underlying principles of their teaching concerning it are unaffected by this; and it is the expression of these underlying principles with which we have to deal.

In Amos v. 16-18, 20, we read as follows: *Therefore thus said the Lord, the God of hosts, the Lord: Wailing shall be in all the broad ways; and they shall say in all the*

the words of Scripture themselves are read. It has therefore been thought well, in spite of the space taken up, to show by quotations how the roots of the Gospel teaching concerning the subject under consideration are embedded in the Old Testament writings.

[1] Sometimes the "Day" is used in a wide sense for the new era itself.

streets, Alas! alas! and they shall call the husbandman to mourning, and such as are skilful of lamentation to wailing. And in all vineyards shall be wailing: for I will pass through the midst of thee, saith the Lord. Woe unto you that desire the day of the Lord! Wherefore would ye have the day of the Lord? it is darkness, and not light. . . . Shall not the day of the Lord be darkness, and not light? even very dark, and no brightness in it? See, too, viii. 9, 10. Two points are noticeable here regarding the signs which precede the end; sorrow and lamentation among men, and the terror of darkness in the physical world; the reiteration of this latter phenomenon emphasises the fact of its inspiring *fear*. In Isa. viii. 21, 22, we have a passage which is eschatological in form and thought, though the immediate context in which it stands has nothing to do with the "last things"; it contains, however, to a large extent, the same notes as those which occur in the Amos passage: *And they shall pass through it, hardly bestead and hungry: and it shall come to pass, that, when they shall be hungry, they shall fret themselves, and curse by their king and by their God, and turn their faces upward. And they shall look unto the earth; and behold distress and darkness, the gloom of anguish; and into thick darkness they shall be driven away.* Although the text is a little ambiguous here in parts, it is clear that we have the same combination of thought, viz., sorrow among men and darkness in the physical world, as was found in the Amos passage, which is unquestionably eschatological. More pointed and much richer in detail is Isa. xiii. 6-16: *Howl ye; for the day of the Lord is at hand; as destruction from the Almighty shall it come. Therefore shall all hands be feeble, and every heart of man shall melt; and they shall be dismayed; pangs and sorrows shall take hold of them; they shall be in pain as a woman in travail; they shall be amazed one at another; their faces shall be faces of flame. Behold, the day of the Lord cometh, cruel, with wrath and fierce anger, to make the land a desolation, and to destroy the sinners thereof out of it. For the stars of heaven and the constellations thereof shall not give their light: the sun shall be darkened in his going forth, and the moon shall not cause her light to shine. . . . Therefore I will make the heavens to tremble, and the earth shall be shaken out of her place, in the wrath of the Lord of hosts, and in the day of his fierce anger. . . . Every one that is found shall be thrust through; and every one that is taken shall fall by the sword. Their infants also shall be dashed in pieces before their eyes; their houses shall be spoiled, and their wives ravished.*

It is clear from the context that these words were uttered in reference to historical events, the doom of Babylon being foremost in the prophet's mind; but the eschatological *traits* contained in the passage had evidently long before this period assumed a stereotyped character, for the same distinguishing marks recur again and again in passages of varied contents and of different ages. That which stands out clearly in the passage before us is the same as in the two other passages already quoted—anguish and sorrow among men, and darkness and other terrifying phenomena in the physical world—only here the words are more striking owing to the wealth of detail. The same thoughts are expressed in a somewhat different way in Isa. xxiv. 23; the preceding verses here tell of the punishment of the proud in the day of the Lord, it then goes on to say: *Then the moon shall be confounded, and the sun ashamed; for the Lord of hosts shall reign in Mount Zion.* In Zeph. i. 14-16, the same *traits* appear, but in this passage, again, the eschatological ideas are connected with, and adapted to, definite historical events; *The great day of the Lord is near, it is near and hasteth greatly, even the voice of the day of the Lord: the mighty man crieth there bitterly. That day is a day of wrath, a day of trouble and distress, a day of wasteness and desolation, a day of darkness and gloominess, a day of clouds and thick darkness. A day of the trumpet and alarm, against the fenced cities, and against the high battlements.* The way in which the stereotyped conceptions concerning the "Day of the Lord" are utilised and applied to present conditions is well illustrated in this passage, where the oft-recurring description of the "darkness" of that Day is followed by reference to a siege. But the most striking details concerning the signs of the "Day of the Lord" are to be found in Joel ii. 1ff.; while we have here a further example of adaptation to present circumstances, the description of eschatological *data* shows distinct development: *Blow ye the trumpet in Zion, and sound an alarm in my holy mountain: let all the inhabitants of the land tremble: for the day of the Lord cometh, for it is nigh at hand; a day of darkness and gloominess, a day of clouds and thick darkness, as the dawn spread upon the mountains; a great and strong people, there hath not been ever the like, neither shall be any more after them, even to the years of many generations. A fire devoureth before them; and behind them a flame burneth. . . . The appearance of them is as the appearance of horses; and as horsemen so do they run. Like the noise of the chariots on the tops of the mountains do they leap, like the noise of a flame of fire that devoureth the stubble, as a strong people set in battle array. At their presence the peoples are in anguish: all faces are waxed pale. . . . The earth quaketh before them; the heavens tremble; the sun and the moon are darkened, and the stars withdraw their shining: and the Lord uttereth his voice before his army; for his camp is very great; for he is strong that executeth his work; for the day of the Lord is great and very terrible; and who can abide it?* And in verses 30, 31, of the same chapter: *And I will show wonders in the heavens and in the earth, blood and fire, and pillars of smoke. The sun shall be turned into darkness, and the moon into blood, before the great and terrible day of the Lord come.* And, once more, in Joel iii. 15, 16, we find for the third time in a short book the description of the darkening of the heavenly bodies: *The sun and the moon are darkened, and the stars withdraw their shining. And the Lord shall roar from Zion, and utter his voice from Jerusalem; and the heavens and the earth shall shake. . . .* These Joel passages show with great distinctness the way in which eschatological teaching is combined with prophecies about the Jewish nation which are prompted by present historical conditions. It is important to bear the fact of this combination in mind; it is characteristic of the writings of all those prophets who give expression to these eschatological conceptions; and since the prophets attach them to a large variety of different historical conditions belonging to periods far apart from each other, the conclusion is forced upon us that we must recognise in Old Testament Eschatology a body of beliefs which were common property, belonging to no *one* age, and evidently of very considerable antiquity. How ancient these beliefs were, may be seen from the fact that the expression "Day of the Lord," which according to Hebrew usage sums up and includes the whole cycle of eschatological conceptions, appears as a well-known *terminus technicus* the first time it occurs in the Old Testament, viz., Amos v. 18.

Moreover, there are grounds for believing that the eschatological material presented to us in the Old Testament constituted a body of *popular beliefs* long current among the people before the prophets took them over and utilised them for the purpose of inculcating higher beliefs. As to the origin of these popular beliefs, this is not the place to discuss the question;[1] it is sufficient for us to note the use made of them by the prophets, for, as far as we are at present concerned, it is the prophetical basis which is our starting-point. Even in the history of eschatological beliefs, as contained in the Old Testament, it is by no means always possible to trace each step in the development of ideas, a fact which seems to indicate that side by side with the prophetic teaching on the subject popular notions also went on developing. An example of this may be seen in the part played by Elijah in the popular conception of later days; nowhere in the Old Testament is there any record as to how it came about that the person of Elijah became an element in eschatological teaching — though it is reasonable to suppose that the account in 2 Kings ii. was the starting-point in this—yet he figures

[1] See the writer's book referred to above, pp. 241ff.

suddenly in connection with the "Day of the Lord" in Mal. iv. 5: *Behold, I will send you Elijah the prophet before the great and terrible day of the Lord come.* Our Lord showed (Matt. xi. 14, xvii. 10-13) that, taken in the literal sense in which it was originally intended to be taken, this eschatological *trait* was erroneous. But the point is both interesting and important, as it shows the possibility of the existence of other *popular* elements which are not recorded in the Old Testament, but which are perhaps still preserved in portions of the Apocalyptic literature (see below, chap. vi.). So much then for some Old Testament examples of the signs which are to precede the End.

§ii. *The Advent of Jehovah, the Judge.*

It is not always possible to keep the details of Old Testament teaching on Eschatology, which we are considering under these four heads, entirely apart; the various elements necessarily run into each other to a large extent, being, as they are, so closely connected with each other. Under our present heading attention is to be drawn to some Old Testament references to the central fact of the Eschatological Drama, viz., the Advent of Jehovah. In most cases, though not invariably, Jehovah appears as Judge; thus in Amos v. 17 we read: *I will pass through the midst of thee, saith the Lord;* the preceding verses tell of the wickedness of the people, *e.g.*, verse 12, *For I know how manifold are your transgressions and how mighty are your sins* . . . , and it is for this reason, as the context goes on to show, that Jehovah is about to "pass through the midst" of them, *i.e.*, it is in order, as their Judge, to punish them. The belief in the *personal appearance* of Jehovah is one which must be borne in mind in view of what will be said in future chapters (see too, the section on *Theophanies* below). It is brought out prominently again in Isa. xxiv. 23; the former half of this verse, as already shown above, contains the stereotyped conceptions concerning the signs preceding the Advent, the latter half goes on to say: *For the Lord of hosts shall reign in Mount Zion, and in Jerusalem, and before his ancients gloriously.* The bringing of Zion and Jerusalem into the circle of eschatological ideas is characteristic of a somewhat later development; it recurs in Isa. lxv. 17-19: *For, behold, I create new heavens and a new earth: and the former things shall not be remembered, nor come into mind. But be ye glad and rejoice for ever in that which I create: for, behold, I create Jerusalem a rejoicing and her people a joy. And I will rejoice in Jerusalem, and joy in my people: and the voice of weeping shall be no more heard in her, nor the voice of crying.* The thought is also present in the well-known passage in Mal. iii. 1-3 concerning the Advent: . . . *And the Lord whom ye seek shall suddenly come to his temple, and the messenger of the covenant, whom ye delight in, behold, he cometh, saith the Lord of hosts. But who may abide the day of his coming? And who shall stand when he appeareth? for he is like a refiner's fire, and like fuller's soap.* . . . The earlier conception appears, however, in a passage which is evidently much later than the thought it expresses, Isa. lxvi. 15, 16: *For, behold, the Lord will come with fire, and his chariots shall be like the whirlwind; to render his anger with fury, and his rebuke with flames of fire. For by fire will the Lord plead, and by his sword, with all flesh: and the slain of the Lord shall be many.* Similar to this passage is Nah. i. 3-6: *The Lord hath his way in the whirlwind and in the storm, and the clouds are the dust of his feet.*

He rebuketh the sea, and maketh it dry, and drieth up all the rivers. . . . The mountains quake at him, and the hills melt; and the earth is upheaved at his presence, yea, the world and all that dwell therein. Who can stand before his indignation? and who can abide in the fierceness of his anger? his fury is poured out like fire, and the rocks are broken asunder by him. As in the case of the signs which are to precede the end, so with the central fact of the Advent of Jehovah, its combination with present historical occurrences is characteristic of Old Testament Eschatology. A good example of this is afforded by the opening verses of the book of Micah; the prophecy is taken up against Samaria and Jerusalem on account of their idolatry, and this wickedness is represented as the cause of Jehovah's Advent, so that in the middle of the prophecy familiar eschatological *traits* suddenly appear. The prophecy (Mic. i. ff.) begins: *The word of the Lord that came to Micah . . . which he saw concerning Samaria and Jerusalem. Hear, ye peoples, all of you; hearken, O earth, and all that therein is: and let the Lord God be witness against you, the Lord from his holy temple.* So far we have words which are in the regular prophetic style and in which there is not necessarily any sign of eschatological thought; and if the words of verse 5 followed verse 2 (just quoted) the connection would be perfectly clear, viz.: *For the transgression of Jacob is all this, and for the sins of the house of Israel* . . . .; but the following words of verses 3, 4 intervene: *For, behold, the Lord cometh forth out of his place, and will come down, and tread upon the high places of the earth. And the mountains shall be molten under him, and the valleys shall be cleft, as wax before the fire, as waters that are poured down a steep place.* This, it will be noticed, is one of the regular conceptions descriptive of the coming of Jehovah; its position, therefore, in the midst of an ordinary prophecy illustrates the truth that eschatological conceptions are utilised and adapted by the prophets for special purposes. Another example of this occurs in Zeph. i. 7-10: *Hold thy peace at the presence of the Lord; for the day of the Lord is at hand;* then comes the prophecy of the punishment of the sinners in Jerusalem, and it continues: *And in that day, saith the Lord, there shall be the noise of a cry from the fish gate, and an howling from the second quarter, and a great crashing from the hills;* a little further on, in verse 14, comes again the definite announcement of the Advent of Jehovah: *The great day of the Lord is near, it is near and hasteth greatly, even the voice of the day of the Lord: the mighty man crieth there bitterly.* Zephaniah refers, once more, to this in iii. 8: *Therefore wait for me, saith the Lord, until the day that I rise up to the prey: for my determination is to gather the nations, that I may assemble the kingdoms, to pour upon them mine indignation, even all my fierce anger; for all the earth shall be devoured with the fire of my jealousy.* Examples of other prophetic utterances concerning the Advent of Jehovah are: Joel ii. 1, *Blow the trumpet in Zion, and sound an alarm in my holy mountain; let all the inhabitants of the land tremble: for the day of the Lord cometh, for it is nigh at hand.* Hag. ii. 6, *For thus saith the Lord of hosts: Yet once, it is a little while, and I will shake the heavens, and the earth, and the sea, and the dry land;* ii. 21, 22, *I will shake the heavens and the earth, and I will overthrow the throne of kingdoms, and I will destroy the strength of the kingdoms of the nations;* and once more, Zech. ii. 13, *Be silent, all flesh, before the Lord; for he is waked up out of his holy habitation.* These will be sufficient to illustrate the Old Testament teaching concerning the actual Advent of Jehovah, but see further below, *Theophanies.*

§iii. *The Judgement upon the Wicked.*

This judgement, which belongs inseparably to Old Testament eschatological teaching, is always against the wicked regarded as the enemies of Jehovah; this *trait*, too, is largely conditioned by the historical circumstances of the time. In its earliest form it may reasonably be assumed that the judgement was upon the powers of evil,[1] but this was adopted by the prophets and applied at one time to the wicked within the Israelite nation, at another to the Gentiles, who, as not being the worshippers of Jehovah, were usually regarded as the natural enemies both of the Israelites and of Jehovah, and are thus classed among the wicked. But, as will be seen in the next section, universalistic tendencies sometimes caused a modification of this attitude in regard to the Gentiles. In the passages now to be considered, therefore, both Israelites in some cases, and Gentiles in others, are represented as the objects of divine wrath, whose punishment is to be accomplished at

[1] Cf. *The Evolution of the Messianic Idea,* chap. xiii.

Jehovah's Advent. Amos is again the first to sound these notes; he denounces Israelite and Gentile alike, all are to suffer the just judgement on account of their wicked deeds at the Advent of Jehovah: i. 2, *The Lord shall roar from Zion, and utter his voice from Jerusalem; and the pastures of the shepherds shall mourn, and the top of Carmel shall wither.* The long passage which follows shows a combination of historical events with the prophecies of judgement, but at the base of all lies the thought contained in the verse just quoted that the Advent of Jehovah will bring with it the punishment of the wicked whether they be Gentiles or the people of the Lord; indeed, the guilt of these latter is the greater, according to Amos, since they were the chosen of the Lord: *You only have I known of all the families of the earth: therefore I will visit upon you all your iniquities* (iii. 2). A specific denunciation against the Israelites is contained in v. 18: *Woe unto you that desire the day of the Lord? Wherefore would ye have the day of the Lord? it is darkness, and not light.* These words reveal the existence of a popular, but erroneous, conception of the "Day of the Lord."[1] In

[1] See *The Evolution of the Messianic Idea*, chap. xvi. pp. 241-248.

Isa. viii. 22, there is an evident echo of the belief in the punishment of the wicked in the "Day of the Lord," though it is an adaptation to a particular time and event; the language, however, is unmistakeably eschatological: *And they shall look unto the earth, and behold, distress and darkness, the gloom of anguish; and into thick darkness they shall be driven away;* see, too, xi. 4: *And he shall smite the earth with the rod of his mouth, and with the breath of his lips shall he slay the wicked;* the words occur in the middle of a well-known eschatological passage. Very clear, again, is the thought in Isa. xiii. 9, 11: *Behold, the day of the Lord cometh, cruel, with wrath and fierce anger; to make the land a desolation, and to* [illegible] *the sinners thereof out of it. . . . And I will punish the world for their evil, and the wicked for their iniquity; and I will cause the arrogancy of the proud to cease, and will lay low the haughtiness of the terrible.* This is spoken of in reference to Gentiles; see further Isa. xvii. 9, however, where it is against the wicked in Israel that punishment "in that day" is proclaimed; but that chapter concludes with one of the most graphic passages in the whole Old Testament, and here the doom is pronounced against the Gentiles because of their enmity against the people of God; the words are of such living force that the whole passage must be quoted: *Ah, the uproar of many peoples, which roar like the roaring of the seas; and the rushing of the nations, that rush like the rushing of mighty waters! The nations shall rush like the rushing of many waters; but he shall rebuke them and they shall flee far off and shall be chased as the chaff of the mountains before the wind, and like the whirling dust before the storm. At eventide behold terror; and before the morning they are not. This is the portion of them that spoil, and the lot of them that rob us.* Here again we have the adaptation of eschatological ideas to a particular event. Then again in Isa. xxiv. 21-23 it says: *And it shall come to pass in that day, that the Lord shall punish the host of the high ones on high, and the kings of the earth. And they shall be gathered together, as prisoners are gathered together in the pit, and shall be shut up in the prison, and after many days shall they be punished. Then shall the moon be confounded, and the sun ashamed. . . .*; the verse that follows shows that the whole passage is eschatological; it has been already quoted above. One other passage from this book must be mentioned, as it is of considerable importance in view of the Gospel teaching (see below ix. §iii.); it is lxvi. 22-24: *For as the new heavens and the new earth which I will make, shall remain before me, saith the Lord, so shall your seed and your name remain. And it shall come to pass, that from one new moon to another, and from one sabbath to another, shall all flesh come to worship before me, saith the Lord. And they shall go forth, and look upon the carcases of the men that have transgressed against me; for their worm shall not die, neither shall their fire be quenched; and they shall be an abhorring unto all flesh.* Micah, like Amos, declares the punishment of the chosen people in "that day" equally with the other peoples of the earth; in the eschatological passage already alluded to above, occur these words: . . . *For the transgression of Jacob is all this, and for the sins of the house of Israel.* . . . (Mic. i. 5-9). Nahum, on the other hand, in his "burden" on Nineveh, in that part which is characterised by eschatological *traits*, says: *But with an over-running flood he will make full end of the place thereof, and will pursue his enemies into darkness* (i. 8). Then again, Zephaniah takes up his parable against the land of Judah in the words: *And I will bring distress upon men, that they shall walk like blind men, because they have sinned against the Lord; and their blood shall be poured out as dust, and their flesh as dung. Neither their silver nor their gold shall be able to deliver them in the day of the Lord's wrath; but the whole land shall be devoured by the fire of his jealousy: for he shall make an end, yea a terrible* (or "speedy") *end, of all them that dwell in the land* (i. 17, 18). The prophet's denunciation continues: *Gather yourselves together, O nation that hath no shame; before the decree bring forth, before the day pass as the chaff, before the fierce anger of the Lord come upon you, before the day of the Lord's anger come upon you* (ii. 1, 2; *cf.*, too, iii. 8, 11). In the book of Zechariah we meet with some new elements, though they do not occur here for the first time; the Jewish nation is to be the instrument for punishing the Gentiles in the "last times," though Jehovah Himself will fight for His people against those who attack them. But the prophet goes on to say that the gracious spirit of the Lord will be poured out upon His people so that they will repent of all their wickedness. See, for these thoughts, Zech. xii.; a few citations from this chapter may be given to illustrate what has been said. In verses 2ff. it says: *Behold I will make Jerusalem a cup of reeling unto all the peoples round about, and upon Judah also shall it be in the siege against Jerusalem. And it shall come to pass in that day, that I will make Jerusalem a burdensome stone for all the peoples; all that burden themselves with it shall be sore wounded; and all the nations of the earth shall be gathered together against it. . . . In that day will I make the Chieftains of Judah like a pan of fire among wood, and like a torch of fire among sheaves; and they shall devour all the peoples round about, on the right hand and on the left. . . . And it shall come to pass in that day I will seek to destroy all the nations that come against Jerusalem. And I will pour out upon the house of David, and upon the inhabitants of Jerusalem, the spirit of grace and of supplication. . . .* Then in chap. xiv. the theme is taken up again and somewhat varied: the nations will attack Jerusalem when the day of the Lord comes, and the city will be sacked; *then,* in the words of the prophet, *shall the Lord go forth, and fight against those nations, as when he fought in the day of battle* (verses 1-3). This chapter will come before us again. Lastly, in Mal. iii. 18, iv. 1-3, indiscriminate punishment upon all the wicked is announced when the "Day of the Lord" comes, though primarily, it would seem, the Jews are meant: *Then shall ye return and discern between the righteous and the wicked, between him that serveth God and him that serveth him not. For, behold, the day cometh, it burneth as a furnace; and all the proud, and all that work wickedness, shall be stubble: and the day that cometh shall burn them up, saith the Lord of hosts, and it shall leave them neither root nor branch. . . . And ye shall tread down the wicked; for they shall be ashes under the soles of your feet in the day that I do make, saith the Lord of hosts;* in this last verse the just are spoken of as those who are to annihilate the wicked, that is to say, they are to constitute the army of the Lord, see Joel ii. 11, where this army is again spoken of, but it appears that here the army of the Lord is to be composed of a "great and strong people" (see verse 2) whom the Lord will raise up for the purpose of punishing the wicked in Israel: *And the Lord uttereth his voice before his army; for his camp is very great; for he is strong that executeth his word; for the day of the Lord is great and very terrible.* With what has been said in this section compare chap. v. §iii.

§iv. *The Blessedness of the Righteous.*

What has been already said more than once must be repeated here, namely, that historical conditions are often the point of attachment utilised by the prophets for the purpose of adding teaching concerning the "last things"; it is only by remembering this that we can understand how it is that in one and the same passage clear references to present conditions are found side by side with expressions and prophecies which are as clearly eschatological. An example of this is found in Amos. v.; part of this chapter deals with the wickedness of the house of Israel, but the hope of forgiveness is held out to those who turn from evil and do the will of God; in the very middle of the chapter, however, occur some *traits* which are indisputably eschatological (verses 16-18, 20), while, on the other hand, the last verse runs: *Therefore will I cause you to go into captivity beyond Damascus, saith the Lord, whose name is the God of hosts* —an obvious reference to an historical event about to occur in the near future, but nothing to do with the "last things." This method of the prophets is of the highest importance, for it tended to show the intimate connection that exists between the condition of men hereafter and their present manner of life; it may be true enough that the prophets had but hazy conceptions as to the actual state of the departed, but that did not affect the principle taught of the relationship between man's state here and hereafter, namely, that according as he was loyal and obedient to the ethical demands of Jehovah, or not, here, so was his condition to be one of peace, or the reverse, hereafter. That among the people material notions obtained concerning the time to come, and that even the prophets themselves looked for the reign of Jehovah as something that was to take place on *this* earth, did not in the least interfere with the principle they sought to inculcate; indeed this must have made their teaching more realistic, and therefore more effective. Since those days the conscience of mankind, quickened by the teaching of Christ, has recognised how truly those prophets taught; the expression of the truth may have been inadequate, the belief may have been to some extent erroneous, but the underlying principle is acknowledged by most men to have been a true one.[1]

In the preceding section we saw that one of the main elements of prophetic eschatological teaching was that in the final issue punishment awaited the wicked; in the present section we must see how the converse of this was also part of the teaching of the Old Testament. In the passage just referred to (Amos v.) the presence of eschatological *traits* make it probable that in the mind of the prophet these lay behind *all* his words in this particular prophecy, and therefore it may be assumed that he had in mind the reward of the Righteous in the "Day of the Lord" when he says, in v. 14, 15: *Seek good, and not evil, that ye may live; and so the Lord, the God of hosts, shall be with you, as ye say. Hate the evil, and love the good, and establish judgement in the gate; it may be that the Lord, the God of hosts, will be gracious unto the remnant of Joseph;* then follows the eschatological passage proper quoted in a previous section. There are a number of passages in the book of Isaiah in which the thought of the final Blessedness of the Righteous finds expression; notable

[1] *Cf.* the Gospel teaching of the Kingdom of God, which shows still more pointedly the indissoluble connection between Ethics and Eschatology.

among these is the long passage in iv. 2-6; this speaks of the happy state of the remnant of Israel in the Messianic Age, which follows after the "last things." A few words may be quoted: *In that day shall the branch of the Lord be beautiful and glorious, and the fruit of the land shall be excellent and comely for them that are escaped of Israel. And it shall come to pass, that he that remaineth in Jerusalem shall be called holy, even every one that is written among the living in Jerusalem. . . .* Isaiah's doctrine of the "Remnant"[1] is important in connection with our present subject, for the belief that only a few, comparatively speaking, will deserve the reward of the Righteous in "that day" finds expression both in his writings as well as in those of later prophets; in x. 20ff., for example, he says: *And it shall come to pass in that day that the remnant of Israel, and they that are escaped of the house of Jacob, shall no more again stay upon him that smote them. . . . For though thy people Israel be as the sand of the sea, only a remnant of them shall return; a consumption is determined, overflowing with righteousness.* The ideal picture of the reign of peace, in Isa. xi. 1-9, is, of course, to be the lot of the

[1] See, on this subject, *The Evolution of the Messianic Idea*, chap. xiv. pp. 206ff.

Righteous. The joy of the Righteous is again spoken of in the eschatological passage, Isa. lxv. 17ff.; in verses 18, 19 we read: *But be ye glad and rejoice for ever in that which I create* (*i.e.*, "new heavens and a new earth"): *for, behold, I create Jerusalem a rejoicing, and her people a joy. And I will rejoice in Jerusalem, and joy in my people: and the voice of weeping shall be no more heard in her, nor the voice of crying.* . . . The same thought occurs again in lxvi. 10ff. and in verse 22 of this chapter: *For as the new heavens and the new earth, which I will make, shall remain before me, saith the Lord, so shall your seed and your name remain.* The blessedness of the Righteous in the "Day of the Lord" is further referred to by the prophet Nahum; in i. 7 occur these words: *The Lord is good, a stronghold in the day of trouble; and he knoweth them that put their trust in him;* both the preceding and following verses are of an eschatological character, the words must therefore be regarded as expressive of thoughts belonging to the same cycle of ideas. The same is to be said of Zeph. ii. 3: *Seek ye the Lord, all ye meek of the earth, which have wrought his judgement; seek righteousness, seek meekness: it may be ye shall be hid in the day of the Lord's anger.* Again in the book of Joel a familiar eschatological passage ends thus: *And it shall come to pass, that whosoever shall call on the name of the Lord shall be delivered: for in Mount Zion and in Jerusalem shall be those that escape, as the Lord hath said, and among the remnant those whom the Lord doth call* (ii. 32). The dwelling of Jehovah in Jerusalem among His people after the terrors of "that day" are past is again referred to in Joel iii. 16, 17: *But the Lord will be a refuge unto his people, and a stronghold to the children of Israel. So shall ye know that I am the Lord your God, dwelling in Zion, my holy mountain: then shall Jerusalem be holy. . . .* The constant reference to the actual dwelling of Jehovah in Jerusalem must strike us as somewhat over-bold, for it would be a mistake to suppose that the prophets did not intend this to be understood in a literal sense; it must, however, be remembered that the prophets picture the conditions under which this is to take place as very different from ordinary earthly conditions; it is a "new heaven" and a "new earth" which is to come into existence first; the destruction and obliteration of all evil is likewise to be accomplished before Jehovah's reign on earth commences; so that the idea is not so incongruous as it might appear at first sight. It is true that to localise Jehovah's presence and to restrict it to the capital of the Jewish nation seems somewhat derogatory to the majesty and illimitableness of the Divine Personality; but, after all, what alternative was there? The conceptions about the spiritual world were still far too undeveloped to permit of transferring the kingdom that was to come to the land where, according to the belief of the times, "all things are forgotten"; and it followed that to conceive rightly of the place where Jehovah and His angels dwelt as that wherein the reign of peace and joy was to be, was an impossibility on account of the spiritual conceptions which such a belief required. Even at the present day things are often written—especially in hymns—about what, for the want of a better name, we call "Heaven," which can scarcely be said to denote very high spiritual conceptions about the world to come; so that it is not surprising to find among writers who lived so many centuries ago, and who had not yet received the revelation which came by Christ, a great mixture of materialistic ideas with spiritual thought in the descriptions of the world to come. And being thus restricted by the nature of the case to this earth, it was necessarily to Jerusalem that the prophets looked as that which was to be the centre of the new kingdom which Jehovah was going to establish; this is so self-evident, seeing that the Jews alone were the worshippers of Jehovah, that the point need not be insisted upon further. One or two other passages may be quoted to illustrate this—Zech. xiv. 8-11: *And it shall come to pass in that day, that living waters shall go out from Jerusalem; half of them toward the eastern sea, and half of them toward the western sea, in summer and winter shall it be. And the Lord shall be King over all the earth: in that day shall the Lord be one, and his name one. . . . And men shall dwell therein, and there shall be no more curse; but Jerusalem shall dwell safely.* In Mal. iv. 1, 2, after the announcement of the approach of the "Day" and the destruction of the wicked, it continues: *But unto you that fear my name shall the sun of righteousness arise with healing in his wings.*

These passages will be sufficient to illustrate the prophets' teaching concerning the Blessedness of the Righteous when the signs which are to precede the coming of the "Day of the Lord" have been fulfilled.

Before summing up what has been said in this chapter, some subsidiary points, not altogether unimportant, must be considered.

CHAPTER III.

THE ANTECEDENTS OF THE GOSPEL TEACHING: SOME FURTHER ELEMENTS IN THE OLD TESTAMENT.

BESIDES the four main elements of Old Testament Eschatology dealt with in the preceding chapter, there are some others directly connected with the subject, but not of the same importance; it will be of interest to touch briefly upon these.

§i. *Theophanies.*

There are, broadly speaking, three kinds of Theophanies spoken of in the Old Testament: firstly, those in which God is represented as appearing in human form, *e.g.*, in Gen. xvi. 13, 14, where Hagar is said to have seen God; *And she called the name of the Lord that spake unto her, Thou art a God that seeth me; for she said, Have I even here looked after him that seeth me? Wherefore the well was called Beer-lahai-roi;* or Gen. xviii., where three men, one of whom was Jehovah, appeared to Abraham as he sat at the entrance of his tent; or again, Gen. xxxii. 24-32, the account of Jacob wrestling at Peniel (*I have seen God face to face, and my life is preserved*). Then, in the second place, we meet with another species of Theophany, according to which God appears in human form, but His appearance is in *visions, i.e.*, the manifestation is to the spiritual, not the material sight; examples of this are Num. xxiv. 4, Isa. vi. 1ff., Ezek. i. 1ff., and many others. It is not, however, Theophanies of either of these kinds to which attention is invited in the present connection, but rather to examples of those which may be called the more normal type of Theophany; these describe the Deity as appearing in fire or storm, and the like. For example, in the description of the great Theophany on Mount Sinai (Exod. xix. 16-25) we read of *thunders and lightnings, and a thick cloud upon the mount. . . . And mount Sinai was altogether on smoke, because the Lord descended upon it in fire: and the smoke thereof ascended as the smoke of a furnace, and the whole mount quaked greatly.* The account in Deut. iv., v. is similar; *e.g.*, iv. 11, 12: . . . *And the mountains burned with fire unto the heart of heaven, with darkness, clouds, and thick darkness. And the Lord spake unto you out of the midst of the fire.* . . . (See, further, iv. 33, 36; v. 4; xxxiii. 2.) Again in Judg. v. 4, 5, we read: *Lord, when thou wentest forth out of Seir, when thou marchedst out of the field of Edom, the earth trembled, the heavens also dropped, yea, the clouds dropped water. The mountains flowed down at the presence of the Lord.* But it is in the Psalms that the most vivid descriptions of Theophanies are to be found; no words could be more awe-inspiring than the account given in Ps. xviii. 7-15 of Jehovah's appearance: *Then the earth shook and trembled, the foundations also of the mountains moved and were shaken, because he was wroth. There went up a smoke out of his nostrils, and fire out of his mouth devoured; coals were kindled at it. He bowed the heavens also and came down; and thick darkness was under his feet. . . . He sent out his arrows and scattered them; yea, lightnings manifold, and discomfited them.* . . . The same thoughts recur in Ps. xcvii. 2-5: *Clouds and darkness are round about him . . . a fire goeth before him, and burneth up his adversaries round about. His lightnings lightened the world; the earth saw, and trembled. The hills melted like wax at the presence of the Lord.* (See, further, xlvi. 7; lxxxiii. 14, 15; civ. 32; cxliv. 5, 6.) But not less striking are the prophetical books in the descriptions they contain of Jehovah's appearances. Some of the passages to be cited belong perhaps more strictly to §ii. of the preceding chapter, though, as they do not directly mention the coming of Jehovah in the "last times," they come here as appropriately; but, in any case, there is an undoubted connection of thought between passages which describe Theophanies and those which deal directly with prophecies of the Advent of Jehovah in the "last days." In Isa. xxx. 27, 28, we have this theophanic picture: *Behold, the name of the Lord cometh from far, burning with his anger, and in thick rising smoke; his lips are full of indignation, and his tongue is as a devouring fire; and his breath is an overflowing stream.* (*Cf.* xxxi. 9; xxxiv. 8-10; Mic. i. 6; Nah. i. 6.) Very graphic are the words in Hab. iii. 3-15: *God came from Teman, and the Holy One from Mount Paran. His glory covered the heavens and the earth was full of his praise. And his brightness was as the light; he had rays coming forth from his hand. . . . Before him went the pestilence, and fiery bolts went forth at his feet. . . . the eternal mountains were scattered, the everlasting hills did bow; his goings were as of old . . . The sun and the moon stood still in their habitation, at the light of thine arrows as they went, at the shining of thy glittering spear. . . . Thou didst tread the sea with thine horses, the heap of mighty waters.* Once more, the thought of Jehovah's appearance in fire is thus expressed in Mal. iv. 1: *For, behold, the day cometh, it burneth as a furnace; and all the proud and all that work wickedness, shall be stubble; and the day that cometh shall burn them up, saith the Lord of hosts, that it shall leave them neither root nor branch.* Finally, there is a passage in which the appearance of Jehovah is referred to, but which also contains an element which will come before us again more than once, namely, that at His appearance enmity will arise between relations and friends. This strange phenomenon which, as will be seen later, forms a characteristic feature at the Advent, occurs here apparently for the first time. The passage in question deals, it is true, with a prophecy regarding Egypt; but, as we have already had occasion to remark, the prophets frequently utilise apocalyptic material and adapt it to the historical circumstances of the time: *Behold, the Lord rideth upon a swift cloud, and cometh unto Egypt; and the idols of Egypt shall be moved at his presence, and the heart of Egypt shall melt in the midst of it. And I will stir up the Egyptians against the Egyptians, and they shall fight every one against his brother, and every one against his neighbour; city against city, and kingdom against kingdom* (Isa. xix. 1, 2).

These passages will be sufficient to show that the conceptions as to the manner of the divine appearances — conceptions which evidently date from very early times—must have greatly influenced the thoughts and words of apocalyptic writers, both Biblical and post-Biblical, in their accounts of the "last things." This is a point which needs to be borne in mind in studying the history of eschatological teaching.

§ii. *The Gathering of the Gentiles.*

There are a very large number of passages which speak of the gathering together of the

Gentiles in the "last times"; at first sight some of these passages appear to be contradictory; but if the standpoint of the various writers of them be taken into consideration it will be seen that the Gentiles are regarded from different points of view, and the attitude of these writers towards the Gentiles is the outcome of these different points of view. Thus, some writers regard the Gentiles as altogether bad since they worship idols, and that they are therefore the enemies of Jehovah; for this reason the Gentiles are looked upon only as the objects of divine wrath, and therefore their punishment and destruction are to be consummated in "that day." Other writers, while fully realising that as idolaters the Gentiles are Jehovah's enemies, nevertheless look forward to a time when the conversion of the Gentiles will be brought about, and this will be in the "Day of the Lord"; so that according to these, it will not be punishment and destruction which will come upon the Gentiles in "that day," but a joining together with Israel in the worship of Jehovah, and therefore the showing forth of Him as the God of all the world. The former represent a somewhat narrow nationalism; in their view, Israel, the people of the Lord, and therefore

His chosen ones, is an altogether unique nation, a "peculiar treasure"; between this "chosen seed" and the peoples of the world there can be no community, least of all a community of worship; this is the *Particularist* attitude. The latter represent those who have a wider outlook upon the world; to them Jehovah is not only the God of Israel, but the Lord of the whole earth; they see, indeed, that the Israelite nation is, from a religious point of view, superior to the Gentiles with their multiplicity of gods and their impure forms of worship, but this superiority only makes Israel the fitter instrument for bringing the Gentiles to God; in the "Day of the Lord," therefore, they look for the gathering in of the Gentiles into the one fold; this is the *Universalist* attitude. A characteristic which is common to both attitudes, and which often finds expression, is that for Israel a process of purification is necessary in "that day" before the nation can enter into the joy of the glorious Era that is to follow; and this idea also occurs, as will be seen presently, in respect of the Gentiles. The doctrine of the Remnant, referred to above, expresses this best of all. But, besides those passages which contain the idea, just mentioned, there are some others which describe how that in the "Day of the Lord" the Gentiles shall gather to war against Israel, and shall overcome them, but that after that Jehovah will Himself fight against the Gentiles and utterly annihilate them. The ideas expressed in this last class of passages belong to the *Particularist* type; they are, comparatively speaking, of late date, and are probably due (in part, at least) to historical conditions; they will come before us again later on.

What has been said must now be briefly illustrated by a few quotations. As an instance of the destruction of the Gentiles Isa. xiii. is instructive, for here is described the final destruction of Babylon, which may be regarded as the enemy of Israel (and therefore of Israel's God) *par excellence*: *The noise of a multitude in the mountains, like as of a great people; the noise of a tumult of the kingdoms of the nations gathered together: the Lord of hosts mustereth the host for the battle. . . . Howl ye, for the day of the Lord is at hand; as destruction from the Almighty shall it come. Therefore shall all hands be feeble, and every heart of man shall melt; and they shall be dismayed; pangs and sorrows shall take hold of them; they shall be in pain as a woman in travail; they shall be amazed one at another; their faces shall be faces of flame* . . . (verses 4-8; *cf.* the whole chapter, especially verses 11, 13, 19, etc.). More general is Isa. xxxiv. 1-4: *Come near, ye nations, to hear, and hearken, ye peoples; let the earth hear, and the fulness thereof; the world, and all things that come forth of it. For the Lord hath indignation against all the nations, and fury against all their host. . . . And all the host of heaven shall be dissolved, and the heavens shall be rolled together as a scroll.* Edom is then, in the following verses, singled out as the especial object of God's wrath: in verse 8 it continues: *For it is the day of the Lord's vengeance* . . . ; these last words show that the passage is an eschatological one. Similar to this is Isa. lxiii. 4-6, where Edom is again mentioned by name, though the peoples generally are included: *For the day of vengeance is in mine heart, and the year of my redeemed is come. . . . And I will tread down the peoples in mine anger, and make them drunk in my fury, and I will pour out their lifeblood on the earth.* One other passage of this type may be given (Zeph. iii. 8): *Therefore wait for me, saith the Lord, until the day that I rise up to the prey:*

for my determination is to gather the nations, that I may assemble the kingdoms, to pour out upon them mine indignation, even all my fierce anger; for all the earth shall be devoured with the fire of my jealousy. This passage, however, leads on to the second type, the *Universalistic* attitude, for it continues in the next verse: *For then will I turn to the peoples a pure language, that they may all call upon the name of the Lord, to serve him with one consent.* A passage of a still more pronounced *Universalistic* character is Isa. ii. 2-4 (=Mic. iv. 1-3): *And it shall come to pass in the latter days, that the mountain of the Lord's house shall be established in the top of the mountains, and shall be exalted above the hills; and all nations shall flow unto it. And many peoples shall go and say, Come ye, and let us go up to the mountain of the Lord, to the house of the God of Jacob; and he will teach us of his ways, and we will walk in his paths* . . . . This community of worship between Israel and the Gentiles in the "latter days" is again referred to in Isa. xi. 12: *And he* (Jehovah) *shall set up an ensign for the nations, and shall assemble the outcasts of Israel, and gather together the dispersed of Judah from the four corners of the earth;* that this is an eschatological passage may be seen from the opening words of the section: *And it shall come to pass in that day. . . .* Another striking passage of the *Universalistic* type is Isa. lxvi. 18: *The time cometh that I will gather all nations and tongues; and they shall come and shall see my glory.* (See, further, Isa. xlv. 20, 22, and others.) Lastly, a passage may be given from one of the visions of Zechariah: *Sing and rejoice, O daughter of Zion: for lo, I come, and I will dwell in the midst of thee, saith the Lord. And many nations shall join themselves to the Lord in that day, and shall be my people* (ii. 10, 11).

Two passages must now be referred to which tell of the gathering together of the Gentiles for the purpose of attacking Israel, but they are finally destroyed through the intervention of Jehovah Himself. The first is Ezek. xxxviii. 14 - xxxix. 16: *Therefore, son of man, prophesy, and say unto Gog, Thus saith the Lord; In that day when my people Israel dwelleth securely, shalt thou not know it? And thou shalt come from thy place out of the uttermost parts of the north, thou, and many peoples with thee, all of them riding upon horses, a great company and a mighty army; and thou shalt come up against my people*

Israel, as a cloud to cover the land. . . . And it shall come to pass in that day, when Gog shall come against the land of Israel, saith the Lord God, that my fury shall come up into my nostrils. . . . And I will plead against him with pestilence and with blood; and I will rain upon him, and upon his hordes, and upon the many peoples that are with him, an overflowing shower, and great hailstones, fire and brimstone. . . . And I will send a fire upon Magog, and on them that dwell securely in the isles . . . This great conflict between the Gentiles gathered together under Gog and Magog, and the nation of Israel in the first place, and then, after Israel's defeat, between Jehovah and the Gentiles, when the latter are annihilated —is one of the most striking elements in the Eschatological Drama. While starting from the historical conditions of the time, and in fact always based on these in the first instance, the war of Gog and Magog with Jehovah represents the idea of the final conflict between the powers of good and evil; it was always the great heathen world-powers which were especially thought of as representing evil; in Ezekiel's prophecy, Persia, Cush and Put are mentioned by name (xxxviii. 5); in the time of the Maccabees the representative oppressive heathen power was the Syrian-Greek empire of Antiochus Epiphanes; and later on, when this disappeared, its place was taken by Rome. It is Jehovah Who is described as gathering together the heathen powers for the conflict; and the defeat of Israel, prior to the destruction of the Gentiles, probably expresses the purificatory process whereby Israel is made fit to inherit the Messianic kingdom which is to be inaugurated after the terrors of "those days." One other passage may be cited to illustrate this; it is Zech. xiv. 1-11: *Behold, the day of the Lord cometh, when thy spoil shall be divided in the midst of thee. For I will gather all the nations against Jerusalem to battle; and the city shall be taken, and the houses rifled. . . . Then shall the Lord go forth, and fight against those nations, as when he fought in the day of battle. . . . And the Lord shall be king over all the earth. . . . And men shall dwell therein, and there shall be no more curse; but Jerusalem shall dwell safely.*

§iii. *The Ingathering of Israel.*

This is so obvious an element of the subject which we are considering, that only a very brief reference need be made to it. The passage which seems to have been especially influential in forming the ideas of later writers on this point is Isa. xxvii. 13: *And it shall come to pass in that day, that a great trumpet shall be blown; and they shall come which were ready to perish in the land of Assyria, and they that were outcasts in the land of Egypt; and they shall worship the Lord in the holy mountain at Jerusalem.* The same type of prophecy occurs in Isa. xi. 11: *And it shall come to pass in that day, that the Lord shall set his hand again the second time to recover the remnant of his people which shall remain, from Assyria, and from Egypt . . . and from the islands of the sea.* (See also Isa. xxxv. 8-10; Mic. vii. 12; Zech. x. 6-11.) Some passages are noteworthy as anticipating that the Gentiles will themselves escort the scattered Israelites back (see Isa. xliv. 22, lx. 4-9, lxvi. 20, and others). So that the ingathering of the dispersed Israelites became a regular and permanent feature in the picture of the "last times." The thought of Israel's ingathering being connected with the purification of the nation has already been alluded to.

§iv. *The Resurrection of the Dead.*

A belief in the Resurrection of the Dead in the "last days" is an integral part of Jewish eschatological teaching. The earliest witness to this belief is apparently Isa. xxvi. 19, a difficult verse, the meaning of which is not brought out with sufficient clearness in the R.V. rendering, which we give, however: *Thy dead shall live; my dead bodies shall arise. Awake and sing, ye that dwell in the dust: for thy dew is as the dew of herbs, and the earth shall cast forth the dead.* The writer, who speaks in the name of the people, looks forward to the setting up of the kingdom, with a strong city, whose walls and bulwarks are salvation, and whose gates will be entered by "a righteous nation" (xxvi. 1ff); and since the nation is but few, the righteous dead shall rise and share the blessedness of the regenerate nation (xxvi. 19). This notable verse should, with Duhm and Cheyne, be read as follows: *Thy dead men* (Israel) *shall arise; the inhabitants of the dust shall awake and shout for joy; for a dew of lights is thy dew, and the earth shall bring to life the Shades.*[1] Most

[1] Charles in *Encycl. Bibl.* ii. 1354.

likely based on this passage is Dan. xii. 2, 3: *And many of them that sleep in the dust of the earth shall awake, some to everlastimg life and some to shame and everlasting contempt. And they that be wise shall shine as the brightness of the firmament; and they that turn many to righteousness as the stars for ever and ever.* The mention here of the resurrection of the wicked implies a great development of belief since Isa. xxvi. was written. An idea which later on doubtless gave a further impulse to the doctrine of the Resurrection was that those who suffered martyrdom for the Law were worthy to share in the future glories of Israel. In the crudest form of the doctrine, the Resurrection was confined to the Holy Land—those buried elsewhere would have to burrow through the ground to Palestine—and to Israelites. The trumpet-blast which was to be the signal for the ingathering of the exiles would also rouse the sleeping dead.[1]

§v. *The Messianic Banquet.*

This point is interesting, but not important;

[1] *Cf.* Oesterley and Box, *The Religion and Worship of the Synagogue*, p. 224.

it is only mentioned here because it is referred to in the Gospels (see below) in a spiritualised form. In Zeph. i. 7, we have a reference to this: *Hold thy peace at the presence of the Lord God; for the day of the Lord is at hand; for the Lord hath prepared a sacrifice, he hath sanctified his guests.* The ideas concerning this Banquet were greatly developed in later times: according to Rabbinical teaching the righteous are to feed on Leviathan (see Isa. xxvii. 1) when the new kingdom—the kingdom of the Messiah—is established.

We shall have occasion to revert to this subject again.

SUMMARY OF THE OLD TESTAMENT TEACHING.

It will be useful now, before we proceed, to gather up the main points of what has been said regarding the Eschatology of the Old Testament.

Everything centres round the "Day of the Lord," which heralds the end of the present conditions on earth and is to inaugurate a new era. This "Day" is referred to often as the "last times," and is to be preceded by certain signs, namely, terrifying phenomena in the heavens, darkness on earth, sorrow and lamentation among men, wars, enmity among friends and relations, and the general break-up of society. The central figure in that "Day" is Jehovah, Whose Advent as Judge is then to be looked for; He will come and set up His Kingdom on Mount Zion, and will renovate all things. Sometimes, however, the central figure is the Messiah, who is to appear as God's representative; this conception comes more and more to the fore as time goes on. There is to be a forerunner, who is to be the prophet Elijah, and he will come to warn the people of the Messiah's near approach. When the actual Advent takes place, the first act of the Judge will be to pronounce the condemnation of the Wicked, who are the enemies of Jehovah. On the other hand, the Righteous will be blest, and peace and happiness is to be their lot. Two tendencies, the Particularistic and the Universalistic, are observable; according to the former, the Gentiles are regarded as altogether outside the pale of Divine mercy, and they have therefore nothing to look forward to in the "last times" but eternal punishment; according to the latter, Jehovah is not merely the God of Israel, but of the whole earth, and *whosoever* obeys Him, even though it be late in the day, will be numbered among the Blessed. And not only so, but the Israelites themselves, though they are the "Chosen People," will only be received into the Kingdom that is to be set up if they have proved themselves worthy. Not infrequently the prophets declare that owing to the wickedness of the nation, it is only a "Remnant" that shall be saved in that day.

It was pointed out more than once that the historical conditions of the time often furnished a point of attachment for eschatological teaching; this important point must be constantly borne in mind.

Then, besides these four main elements, there were some others which required a passing notice. It was pointed out that the normal type of Theophany in the Old Testament—that, namely, which describes the Deity as appearing in fire and storm, and the like—must be taken into consideration in studying the antecedents of the eschatological teaching of the Gospels. Secondly, the gathering of the Gentiles in the "last times" was shown to be a regular feature in Old Testament Eschatology; here again the two attitudes of thought referred to above come into evidence; on the one hand, this gathering of the Gentiles is declared to be merely a preliminary to their final destruction ; on the other, it is in order that they may be gathered into the fold of the Righteous. Sometimes the nation of Israel is designated as being the medium for bringing the Gentiles to God. Thirdly, the ingathering of Israel became, in the later prophetical literature, a regular and permanent feature of the "last times." A belief in the Resurrection is at least adumbrated in the two passages, Isa. xxvi. 19; Dan. xii. 2, 3. And lastly, the idea of a Messianic Banquet was likewise seen to be probably referred to in Zeph. i. 7.

According to the Old Testament presentment of the Eschatological Drama, it is on this earth that it all takes place, and the Kingdom to be established is likewise of this world; at the same time, some supernatural *traits* seem to foreshadow more spiritual ideas.

CHAPTER IV.

THE ANTECEDENTS OF THE GOSPEL TEACHING. THE APOCALYPTIC LITERATURE: INTRODUCTORY.

OLD Testament Eschatology forms the foundation upon which the Apocalyptic writers based their speculations, in the first instance; and, as will be seen, these writers repeat and develop the conceptions and prophecies which have been epitomised under the various headings in the preceding chapters. But before we come to examine in some little detail the eschatological contents of their writings, it may be well, firstly, to offer some general remarks upon the Apocalyptic literature as a whole, and, secondly, to enumerate the books from which the material to be utilised is taken.

It is important to remember that the Apocalyptic literature as a whole is a *popular* literature; that is to say, it reflects the thoughts of religious circles which were outside the recognised Rabbinical schools; and it embodies religious ideas which in many points sharply conflicted with the strict scholastic orthodoxy of the Pharisees. The main energies of the latter were devoted to the development of the "Oral tradition," in order to build a hedge around the Law,[1] and fix a sharp line of demarcation between Israel and the outside world. The Apocalyptists, on the other hand, though loyal to the Law, did not make it their exclusive preoccupation. They were much more deeply interested in "transcendental Messianism," and in speculative schemes regarding the "end" of the age, and all that such involved. On the other hand, orthodox Rabbinic Judaism—which represents the triumph of the Pharisaic party within the ranks of Judaism—practically banned the entire Apocalyptic literature. Nevertheless, Apocalyptic teaching profoundly influenced orthodox Judaism in some respects. These writings emphasise the individual side of religion equally with that of the righteous community; not the nation as such, but the

[1] "Make a fence to the Torah" (*Pirqe Aboth*, i. 1), which Dr Taylor, in his edition of the work, paraphrases in the words: "Impose additional restrictions so as to keep at a safe distance from the forbidden ground."

community of the righteous within it—the "plant of righteousness," as it is called in the *Book of Enoch*—will inherit the divine reward; the influence of prophetic teaching is very plainly visible here. The exalted religious scheme which dominates these books tended to overcome national and Particularistic limitations; and here certain of the prophetical writers have their successors in the Apocalyptists. It is, however, on the side of the Messianic hope that this literature is most significant; and here the points of contact, as will be seen later on, are most striking and important. Another noteworthy characteristic is its supernatural colouring; in the place of the old antithesis, *present* and *future*, it substitutes that of *above* and *below*. It thus acquires an "other-worldliness" which was in marked contrast to the strictly practical and narrow purview of scholastic Pharisaism, and formed a distinct advance towards the lofty spirituality of the New Testament.[1] Herein, once more, prophetical influence is seen to be asserting itself. But there is another feature in this literature which is of the highest importance; in the words of Professor Charles:

[1] *Cf.* Oesterley and Box, *op. cit.* pp. 34, 211.

"The object of Apocalyptic literature in general was to solve the difficulties connected with a belief in God's righteousness and the suffering condition of his servants on earth. The righteousness of God postulated the temporal prosperity of the righteous, and this postulate was accepted and enforced by the Law. But while the continuous exposition of the Law in the post-exilic period confirmed the people in their monotheistic faith and intensified their hostility to heathenism, their expectations of material well-being, which likewise the Law had fostered, were repeatedly falsified, and a grave contradiction thus emerged between the old prophetic ideals, and the actual experience of the nation, between the promises of God and the bondage and persecution which the people had daily to endure at the hands of their pagan oppressors. The difficulties arising from this conflict between promise and experience might be shortly resolved into two, which deal respectively with the position (1) of the righteous as a community, and (2) of the righteous man as an individual. The Old Testament prophets had concerned themselves chiefly with the former, and pointed in the main to the restoration (or 'resurrection') of Israel as a nation, and to Israel's ultimate possession of the earth as a reward of righteousness. Later, with the growing claims of the individual, and the acknowledgment of these in the religious and intellectual life, the second problem pressed itself irresistibly on the notice of the religious thinkers, and made it impossible for any conception of the divine rule and righteousness which did not render adequate satisfaction to the claims of the righteous individual to gain acceptance. Thus, in order to justify the righteousness of God, there was postulated not only the resurrection of the righteous nation but also the resurrection of the righteous individual. Apocalyptic literature, therefore, strove to show that, in respect alike of the nation and of the individual, the righteousness of God would be fully vindicated; and, in order to justify its contention, it sketched in outline the history of the world and of mankind, the origin of evil and its course, and the final consummation of all things; and thus, in fact, it presented a Semitic philosophy of religion."[1]

Now it is clear that when, in days gone by, men spoke and wrote about what was going to take place at the end of the world, their utterances must have been either of the nature of prophecy or speculation; in either case they believed that they were the recipients of Divine communications; it was God, they were convinced, who was according them

[1] Professor Charles in *Encycl. Bibl.* i. 213, 214.

revelations of things that were to be. Their visions of the "last things" were thus "Apocalyptic" visions, *i.e.*, the uncovering, or revealing, through divine agency, of what was going to happen at the end of the world. By the time of the New Testament period the great body of eschatological ideas was fully developed; these ideas, though in their germ reaching back to the earliest prophetical times, matured and became more or less crystallised during the two eventful centuries that immediately preceded the rise of Christianity. It was these centuries which saw the unfolding and rich growth of the *Apocalyptic Movement* with its vast eschatological developments, the antecedents of which we have sought to indicate in the preceding chapters; and, as we have seen, the literature which was the outcome of this *Movement* was popular in character. It is worth while to try and realise for a moment the importance and significance of these two facts. If this Apocalyptic literature had thus been in the making during the two centuries preceding the Advent of Christ, the Jewish nation, as a whole, must have been familiar with at least the central ideas with which it dealt. It is well known that the people looked for the "Restoration of Israel"[1] when the Messiah should come, and believed that at His appearing their hopes regarding an ideal future would be realised; but this expectation and these hopes had been formulated and fostered by the Apocalyptists, basing much of their teaching, of course, upon the prophetical literature; the result was that owing to this Apocalyptic literature, the nation had been prepared for the coming of the Messiah. But another point of high importance is that our Lord Himself must have been familiar, at all events, with the essential points with which this literature dealt. It was said just now that the Apocalyptic literature was one which reflected the thoughts of religious circles which were outside the recognised Rabbinical schools, and that much which it taught conflicted with the strict scholastic orthodoxy of the Pharisees; the main reason of this was because in this Apocalyptic literature the outlook was wider, the atmosphere was freer, and there was none of that narrow, circumscribed, hair-splitting legalism, which other authorities besides the Gospels have taught us to connect with Pharisaism. The antagonism of the Pharisees towards our Lord must have been in part due to His eschato-

[1] *Cf.* Luke ii. 38.

logical teaching, and this must also have been *one* of the reasons why the people clung to Him and followed Him; for it must be remembered that as soon as they looked upon Him as the Messiah, they would connect with Him all the current ideas regarding the end of the world.

The Apocalyptic writings with which we are specially concerned here are the following:—

The "Ethiopic" Book of Enoch. This book is composite in character; in it are incorporated several works by different authors and of different dates. The following table shows the various elements which the book contains with their approximate dates:—

"The Book of Enoch," chaps. i.-xxxvi. (170 B.C.); lxxxiii.-xc. (166-161 B.C.); xci.-civ. (134-95 B.C.)

"The Book of Celestial Physics," chaps. lxxii.-lxxxii. (166-161 B.C.).

"The Book of Similitudes," chaps. xxxvii.-lxx. (94-64 B.C.).

"The Apocalypse of Noah," extracts from this work are interspersed throughout the above. This Apocalypse is referred to in *The Book of Jubilees*, x. 13, 14, xxi. 10; its date is uncertain, but it was undoubtedly written before the commencement of the Christian Era.

There are also many interpolations, some from Christian sources, in the book.

The name "*Ethiopic*" *Book of Enoch* is given because the earliest version of the work which has been preserved is the Ethiopic. It only represents part of the "Enoch literature," which must at one time have been voluminous. The importance of this book will be seen when it is realised that, in the words of Professor Charles, "all the writers of the New Testament were familiar with it, and were more or less influenced by it in thought and diction. It is quoted as a genuine production of Enoch by St Jude, and as Scripture by St Barnabas. The authors of *The Book of Jubilees, The Apocalypse of Baruch* and *The Fourth Book of Esdras* laid it under contribution. With the earlier Fathers and Apologists it had all the weight of a canonical book, but towards the close of the third and the beginning of the fourth centuries it began to be discredited, and finally fell under the ban of the Church."[1]

In the quotations from this work which will be given below the references are from Professor Charles's edition; it will not be necessary to indicate in each instance from which particular portion the quotation is taken, as a reference to the table given above will show this. The book will be quoted as "Ethiopic Enoch" to

[1] *The Book of Enoch*, pp. 1, 2.

distinguish it from the "Slavonic Enoch" (see below on this latter).

The Sibylline Oracles.—Most of this work is later than the beginning of the Christian Era; the portions with which we are concerned, however, belong probably to the second century B.C.; they are the "Procemium" and Book iii.

The Testaments of the Twelve Patriarchs.—Written between 109-105 B.C. Regarding the use made of this work by New Testament writers, see Charles, in his edition, pp. lxxviii.-xcii.

The Psalms of Solomon.—This work is of composite authorship; the date is approximately 70-40 B.C.

The Book of Jubilees.—A Pharisaic work belonging to about 40-10 B.C.

The Book of the Secrets of Enoch.—This is often referred to as the "Slavonic Enoch" on account of its existing at present only in Slavonic. Though belonging to the once voluminous "Enoch literature," it is quite a distinct work from the "Ethiopic Enoch," spoken of above. It was written by an Alexandrian Jew at the beginning of the Christian Era; but pre-existing material has been largely utilised.

The Ascension of Isaiah.—A book of composite authorship, partly Jewish and partly Christian, the latter being, however, probably based on earlier Jewish work, the earliest portions belong to the very beginning of the Christian Era, the latest to the end of the first century A.D., or somewhat later.

The Assumption of Moses.—The work of a Pharisee, belonging to quite the beginning of the Christian Era; it was written in Palestine.

The Apocalypse of Baruch (Syriac).—A composite work written by Pharisees: though not written till the second half of the first Christian century, it reflects earlier beliefs and ideas, and is of considerable importance in the present connection. It is an entirely different work from the Greek Apocalypse of Baruch.

The Fourth Book of Esdras.—This extremely important Jewish Apocalyptic work belongs to the end of the first Christian century, but it embodies many conceptions of pre-Christian times. In the English Apocrypha it is called the *Second* Book of Esdras, but the more strictly accurate title is as given here.

It will not be inappropriate to append here a selected Bibliography of the above-mentioned works:—

The Book of Enoch (English text 1890, Ethiopic text 1906) edited by R. H. Charles.—The Greek text is published by Dr Swete in *The Old Testament in Greek*, vol. iii. (1899).

The Sibylline Oracles.—Translated from the Greek into English blank verse, with notes (1889), edited by M. S. Terry.

The Testaments of the Twelve Patriarchs (English 1908, Greek text 1908).—Edited by R. H. Charles.

The Psalms of Solomon.—These have been published in Greek and English, under the title "The Psalms of the Pharisees," edited by Ryle and James (1891); the Greek text has also been published by Dr Swete, *op. cit.* pp. 765-787 (1896).

The Book of Jubilees.—Translated from the Editor's Ethiopic text; edited by R. H. Charles (1902).

The Book of the Secrets of Enoch.—Edited by Morfill and Charles (1896).

The Ascension of Isaiah.—Text, translation, and commentary, by R. H. Charles (1900).

The Assumption of Moses.—Text, translation, and commentary, by R. H. Charles (1897).

The Apocalypse of Baruch.—Translated from the Syriac, and edited by R. H. Charles (1896).

The Fourth Book of Esdras (Ezra).—The Latin text has been published by Bensley and James in "Texts and Studies," iii. 2 (1895).

All the above, with the exception of the *Secrets of Enoch*, exist in a German translation, together with Notes, in Kautzsch's *Die Apokryphen und Pseudepigraphen des Alten Testaments*, vol. ii. (1900); the different books are edited by leading German scholars.

CHAPTER V.

THE ANTECEDENTS OF THE GOSPEL TEACHING: THE APOCALYPTIC LITERATURE.

WE must now show by quotations from the Apocalyptic literature that the eschatological teaching of the Old Testament prophets was continued, being both developed and elaborated during the two centuries immediately preceding the Christian Era. The divisions of this chapter will correspond with those of chap. ii., so that the teaching of the two classes of literature may be easily compared. It will be the more necessary to give quotations in full here, owing to the fact that editions of the works belonging to this class of literature are not easily available on account of their cost.

§i. *The Signs which precede the End.*

In *Ethiopic Enoch* i. 5-7 we read that, on the appearance of the Holy and Great One, " every one will be smitten with fear, and the watchers will quake, and great fear and trembling will seize them unto the ends of the earth. And the high mountains will be shaken, and the high hills will be made low, and will melt like wax before the flame. And the earth will be rent and all that is upon the earth will perish . . . . ;" the "watchers" (*'îrîn*) are mentioned for the first time in Dan. iv. 13, 17, 23 (iv. 10, 14, 20 in the Aramaic); in *Slavonic Enoch* xviii. 1 they are called "angels"; strictly speaking, the fallen angels are meant, though in *Ethiopic Enoch* lxxi. 7 "it designates the archangels" (Charles *in loc.*). In later passages of this book similar ideas occur, thus xcix. 4. 5: "In those days (*i.e.* immediately before the Advent of the Messiah) nations shall rise up, and the Kindreds of the Gentiles will lift themselves up on that day of destruction. In that day shall they who suffer want go and hew their children in pieces and cast them away." A "sign" of a different kind is recorded in c. 1, 2: "And in those days the fathers together with their sons will be smitten in one place, brothers will fall in death one with another until it streams with their blood like a river. For a man will not withhold his hand from slaying his sons and his sons' sons, and the sinner will not withhold his hand from his honoured brother: from dawn till sunset they will slay one another." Another characteristic passage is cii. 1, 2: "And in those days when he brings a grievous fire upon you, whither will ye flee and where will ye find deliverance. . . . ? And all the luminaries will quake with direst fear, and all the earth will be affrighted and tremble and be alarmed." In one of the fragments from the *Apocalypse of Noah*, preserved in this book (lxxx. 4-8), we read: "And the moon will alter her order and not appear at her (appointed) time . . . . and many chiefs of the superior stars will err, and these will alter their orbits and tasks, and will not appear at the seasons prescribed to them . . . ." The third book of *The Sibylline Oracles* contains several passages describing the signs of the "last times"; only one or two need be cited here. In verses 71ff. the approach of the terrors of the great God are spoken of, then in 83-85 it goes on to say that the firmament will fall to the earth and into the ocean, and a mighty cascade of fire will flow down incessantly and burn up earth and sea. In verses 184ff. the wickedness of men in those days is described, this being one of the signs of the approaching end; and this will be followed "in those days" by oppression and confusion among men, and the general break-up of society. Among the "signs" that are spoken of in this book are fiery swords which shall fall from heaven upon the earth, and burning torches which will drop among men (verses 669ff.). The most striking passage, however, is the following (verses 796-806): "But I will tell thee of a sure sign whereby thou mayest know when the end of all things is coming upon the earth; when swords appear in the star-lit heavens towards evening and towards morning; then will a dust-storm descend from heaven upon the whole earth, and the splendour of the sun will disappear from the heavens at midday, and the moonbeams will become visible on earth. Another sign will be bloody drops upon rocks; in the clouds ye will see a battle . . . thus God who dwells in the heavens will bring about the end of all things." The teaching of *The Testaments of the Twelve Patriarchs* on this subject may be illustrated by a few quotations; Levi iv. 1 runs: . . . . "When the rocks are being rent, and the sun quenched, and the waters dried up, and the fire cowering, and all creation troubled, and the invisible spirits melting away, and Hades taketh the spoils through the visitations of the Most High, men will be unbelieving and persist in their iniquity." Judah xxii. 1, 2: "And the Lord shall bring upon them divisions one against another. And there shall be continued wars in Israel; and among men of another race shall my kingdom be brought to an end, until the salvation of Israel shall come." That, as in the case of the Old Testament prophets, the Apocalyptic writers often based their eschatological prophecies upon the historical conditions of their own times is what one would expect. Professor Charles remarks on the passage cited: "During the civil wars in the reign of Alexander Jannæus 50,000 Jews are said to have perished. From the death of Alexander to the accession of Herod Palestine was hardly ever free from civil strife." (See, further, Schürer, *The Jewish People in the Time of Jesus Christ*, I. i. pp. 301-307, etc.) In Asher vii. 2, the signs of the coming of the "last times" are thus referred to: "For I know that ye shall sin, and be delivered into the hands of your enemies, and your soul shall be made desolate, and your holy places destroyed, and ye shall be scattered unto the four corners of the earth. And ye shall be set at nought in the dispersion as useless water, until the Most High shall visit the earth. . . ." (*Cf.* also Naph. viii. 1ff.) *The Book of Jubilees* also has several passages which speak of the signs of the "last times," *e.g.*, xxiii. 12ff., where it says that "in those days there will be plague upon plague, wound upon wound, sadness upon sadness, evil rumour upon evil rumour, and many similar terrible punishments, one after another; sickness, destruction, frost, hail, snow, fever, cold, stiffness, drought, death, sword, imprisonment, and every kind of sorrow and sickness. And all this will come upon the evil generation that sins upon the earth. . . ." A long passage of similar content follows; see also xxxvi. 10ff. *The Ascension of Isaiah,* which is to a large extent of Christian origin, evidently, however, utilises much earlier material; a passage from a work called *The Testament of Hezekiah,* which has been incorporated into the *Ascension,*[1] runs: ". . . And at his word the sun will rise at night, and he will make the moon to appear at the sixth hour" (iv. 5.); a description of the Second Advent follows later on. Of more interest, because of its greater details, is a poetic passage in *The Assumption of Moses,* x. 1-10, one of the

[1] See Charles's edition, pp. xxxvi.-xliii.

most striking descriptions of the "last things" which we possess; it tells first of the impending Advent, and then goes on (verses 4-6): "Then shall the earth quake and it shall be shaken unto the ends thereof, and the high mountains shall be brought low, and shall be shaken, and the valley shall sink down. The sun shall no more give her light, and shall be turned into darkness. The horns of the moon shall be broken, and shall be wholly turned into blood. And the course of the stars shall be brought into confusion. The sea shall withdraw into the abyss, and the wells shall cease, and the rivers shall dry up." With these words it will be interesting to compare Isa. ii. 19, xiii. 10; Ezek. xxxii. 7; Joel ii. 10, iii. 4, iv. 15; *Pss. of Sol.* xvii. 21; *Test. xii. Patr.*, Levi iv. 4; *iv. Esdras* vi. 24; *Sib. Orac.* v. 158, 159. The Syriac *Apocalypse of Baruch* has a large amount of material of which only a few selected passages can find a place here; in xxv. 2ff. it says: "This, therefore, shall be the sign (*i.e.*, of the coming of the Most High at the end of the days); numbing fear shall take hold of the inhabitants of the earth, they shall fall into many grievous troubles (*cf.* Dan. xii. 1), yea, shall fall into terrible torments. And when, owing to their great sorrows, they will say in their hearts, 'Give no more thought to the mighty of the earth,' and when they shall give up all hope, then shall that 'time' commence." Chap. xxvii. of this book enumerates the sorrows that are to come upon men in "those days"; there are to be twelve periods into which these sorrows will be divided, each period being characterised by special terrors; the first will initiate the beginning of travail, in the second will follow the murder of the great ones of the earth, in the third the death of many men, in the fourth the sending out of the sword (*cf.* for this expression Jer. xxv. 16, 27), in the fifth hunger and drought, in the sixth revolutions and terrors, in the seventh . . . . (part of the text has fallen out here), in the eighth many apparitions and meetings with demons, in the ninth the falling of fire from heaven, in the tenth robbery and oppression, in the eleventh wicked deeds and self-indulgence, and in the twelfth a repetition and mixing up of all the foregoing. These woes which are to precede the coming of the Messiah are again dealt with in xlviii. 25-41, and in lxx. 2-10. Lastly, in *iv. Esdras* a long account of these "signs" is given in chaps. v., vi.; to give but one or two passages out of many: "Then shall the sun shine suddenly at night-time, and the moon in the day-time; blood will flow down from the trees; the stones will cry aloud; the nations shall rise up. . . . In many places abysses will open up, and fire will break forth; the wild beasts will leave their haunts; women will bear mis-shapen monsters; sweet water will turn salt; friends will suddenly fight against one another" (v. 4-9). Very important, too, in this connection is ix. 1ff.: ". . . And when thou seest that a part of the signs which have been announced are past, then wilt thou understand that the time has come in which the Most High will punish the earth that He has created, when there shall appear in the world:

> Revolution in the lands,
> Disquietude among the peoples,
> Devices of the nations,[1]
> Fightings among princes,
> Enmity among rulers,[2]—

then wilt thou understand that these are the things that the Most High spoke of since the days which were from the beginning. . . ." See the whole passage, which is very suggestive all through.

[1] *Cf.* Ezek. xxxviii. 10.
[2] The poetic form of these lines suggests ancient material.

§ii. *The Advent of Jehovah the Judge.*

The thought of the end of the age and that of the actual Advent belong of course together, one presupposes the other; and therefore we shall not expect to find in every passage dealing with the approach of God, or of the Messiah,[1] the direct statement that this approach heralds the end of all things; nor shall we expect to find in every passage dealing with the "end of the age" a direct statement of the actual Advent. The whole cycle of eschatological ideas—and this cannot be too strongly insisted upon—was public property, and therefore very familiar to the people in general; the vast mass of eschatological literature which must once have existed illustrates this fact. We must now deal with a few passages which embody the two ideas of the "end of the age" and of the actual Advent, the preceding signs of which have been referred to in the foregoing section. These may be prefaced by a few words from the book of Daniel; this book exercised a good deal of influence on the Apocalyptic literature, of

[1] On this point see *The Evolution of the Messianic Idea*, pp. 236ff.

which (so far as we know) it is the earliest example in the stricter sense. In Dan. viii. 19, we read: *And he said, Behold, I will make thee know what shall be in the latter time of the indignation; for it belongeth to the appointed time of the end* (*cf.* the visions in chaps. vii., viii.). More pointed is xi. 40, where again historical conditions form the basis of eschatological thought: *And at the time of the end shall the king of the south contend with him; and the king of the north shall come against him like a whirlwind, with chariots, and with horsemen, and with many ships; and he shall enter into the countries, and shall overflow and pass through.* The reference here is evidently to the "end of the age," both from the opening expression, as well as on account of the words which come later on and belong to the same passage: *And there shall be a time of trouble such as never was since there was a nation.* The actual appearing of the Almighty is spoken of in *Eth. Enoch* i. 3, 4, 9: "Concerning the elect I spake, and uttered a parable concerning them: the Holy and Great One will come forth from His dwelling, the God of the world. And going from thence He will tread on Mount Sinai and appear with His hosts, and in the strength of His might appear from

Heaven. . . . And lo! He comes with ten thousands of (His) holy ones to execute judgement upon them . . . . ;" this is from the earliest portion of the book, but *The Book of the Similitudes* also refers to the Advent, *e.g.*, xxxviii. 2: "And when the Righteous One shall appear before the eyes of the elect righteous whose works are wrought in dependence on the Lord of spirits . . . ." See also xxxix. 6: "In that place did mine eyes behold the 'Chosen One' (*i.e.*, the Messiah)[1] of righteousness and faithfulness; in his days shall righteousness reign." So, too, in the other portion of this work, called "The Book of Celestial Physics," the Advent is clearly referred to in the words: "And the Lord of Spirits seated him (*i.e.*, the Messiah) on the throne of his glory and the spirit of righteousness was poured out upon him, and the word of his mouth slew all the sinners, and all the unrighteous were destroyed before his face. And there will stand up in that day all the kings, and the mighty, and the exalted, and those who hold the earth, and they will see and recognise him how he sits on the throne of

[1] See Luke ix. 35: *This is my Son, my chosen; hear ye him;* xxiii. 35: *Let him save himself if this is the Christ of God, his chosen.* (*Cf.* Isa. xliii. 1, 2; *Eth. Enoch* xl. 5; xlv. 3, 4; xlix. 2, 4; li. 3, 5.)

his glory" (lxxii. 2ff.; see the whole chapter); the passage is especially interesting when compared with *The Book of Enoch* proper, for as will have been seen above, in i. 3ff., it is God Himself, the "Holy and Great One," who is the central figure in the Advent, while in the passage just quoted it is the Messiah who takes up this position. One other passage from this portion of the book is worth quoting: "And he sat on the throne of his glory, and the sum of judgement was committed unto him, the Son of Man, and he caused the sinners and those who have led the world astray to pass away and be destroyed from off the face of the earth . . . " (lxix. 27ff.).

Turning now to *The Sibylline Oracles*, we find the expectation of the approach of the "last times" expressed thus: "When will that day come, and the judgement of the immortal God, the Great King? . . . For (that day) shall come in the which the smell of brimstone will be evident to all men" (iii. 55-61). In another passage of this book it is not the immortal God who is to come, but a King whom He will send from Heaven: "And then will God send a King from Heaven to judge each one with blood and the glow of fire. But there is a royal stock, whose seed will not perish, but will in the fulness of time reign and rear up a new Temple of God" (iii. 286-290). A similar passage occurs in iii. 625-658: "And then God will send a King from the rising up of the sun (*i.e.*, from the east) who will put an end to the terrible war on the whole earth, some he will slay, with others he will make a covenant. And this all will he do not by following his own counsel, but by following the righteous purposes of the great God. And the Temple of the great God will stand forth in rich splendour, with gold and silver and purple. . . . " This mention of the Temple is interesting; we shall refer to it again in dealing with the Gospel teaching on the subject. It is spoken of also in a passage in *The Book of Jubilees* i. 29ff.: "And the Angel of the presence who went before the hosts of Israel, took the tables of the divisions of the year . . . from the day of the new creation, when Heaven and earth and all creatures shall be renewed like the powers of the Heavens and like every creature of the earth, until the Sanctuary of God in Jerusalem on Mount Zion shall be made. . . . " (See, further, xxiii. 27ff.) The thought of the "last times" is frequent in *The Testa-*

ments of the Twelve Patriarchs, and, as in the Old Testament, it is, as a rule, present historical conditions which form the point of attachment to which are joined eschatological prophecies; various expressions are used to denote the end, *e.g.*: "the consummation of the times" (Reuben vi. 8); "the end of the ages" (Levi x. 2; Benj. xi. 3); "the last times" (Issachar vi. 1); "the time of consummation" (Zebulon ix. 9), etc. It is by no means always that the Personal appearance of God or the Messiah is specifically mentioned, although this is always understood; herein the *Testaments* are at one with most of the Apocalyptic literature. The mention of God Himself as the Messianic ruler occurs, however, in, *e.g.*, Zebulon viii. 8: "And after these things there shall arise unto you the Lord himself, the light of righteousness, and ye shall see (the place) which the Lord shall choose. Jerusalem is its name." (*Cf.* Mal. iv. 2.) With this should be compared Levi xviii. 2-14, which is also an eschatological passage, but the place of the Almighty is taken by another here: "Then shall the Lord raise up a new priest. And to him all the words of the Lord shall be revealed; and he shall execute a righteous judgement upon the earth for a multitude of days. And his star shall arise in heaven as of a King, lighting up the light of knowledge as the sun the day, and he shall be magnified in the world . . . . ;" but more frequently it is God Himself who is represented as the central figure in the Advent, thus Simeon vi. 5-7: " . . . For the Lord God shall appear on earth, and save the sons of men. . . ." (See also Levi ii. 11, Naphthali viii. 3, and Asher vii. 3.) In this last passage it tells of how the Most High shall visit the earth, coming Himself, and breaking the head of the dragon in the water. These are only a very few passages from this most interesting work. In *The Book of Jubilees* the personality of the central figure at the Advent is not described, but may be inferred from such a passage as xxiii. 29-31, which is eschatological: ". . . And then will God heal his servants . . . and the righteous shall behold and give thanks, and they shall rejoice in all eternity, and shall see all the judgement upon their enemies and all their curse. And their bones shall rest in the earth, and their spirit shall have great joy, and they shall understand that it is God who commands judgement, and who shows mercy upon hundreds and thousands, even upon all that love him." But this book does not offer a great deal which is appropriate in the present connection; the same must be said of *The Ascension of Isaiah*, though here and there some interesting evidence is forthcoming, thus in *The Testament of Hezekiah*, which is incorporated in this book, we read that "the Lord will come with his angels and with the armies of the holy ones from the seventh heaven with the glory of the seventh heaven . . ." (iv. 14ff.); from the same portion of the book the following may also be cited: "And there will be much slander and vain-glory at the approach of the Lord, and the Holy Spirit will withdraw from many" (*cf.* verse 30); this, however, is evidently Christian, though on comparing it with other pre-Christian passages, one can see that it is based on earlier material. Considerably more material is contained in the Syriac *Apocalypse of Baruch*; here we read, for example, in xxix. 1ff: ". . . Then shall the Messiah begin to reveal himself;" in xxx. 3: "For every one knows that the time has come of which it is said that it is the end of the times." But the fullest account in this book is contained in chap. lxxxiii. This begins: "For the Most High shall surely cause his times to come quickly, he shall surely cause his periods to commence; he shall surely judge those who are in his world. . . . But the end of the world shall then show forth the great might of the Ruler, for all men shall be brought to judgement . . ." (see the whole chapter). It is important to note how in this book the limitation in time of the Messianic rule is taught; it is said, for example, in xxx. 1: "And after that, when the time of the Advent of the Messiah has been accomplished, he will return unto heaven in glory." This limited duration seems implied again in xl. 1-4: ". . . And they shall bring him (*i.e.*, the last evil ruler) up to Mount Zion, and my Messiah will question him concerning all his evil deeds, and he will gather together and lay before him all the deeds of his followers. And after that he (*i.e.*, the Messiah) will slay him, but the remnant of my people, even those who are found in the land which I have chosen, will he protect; and his rule shall last continually, for ever, until the world, which is condemned to destruction, comes to an end, and until the times which have been referred to, have been completed." In some respects *iv. Esdras* is the most important among Apocalyptic writings; the Advent of the Messiah is described in xiii. 2-13, which contains the

"Vision of the Man ascending out of the sea"; this passage is sufficiently important to be quoted in full. The following is a translation of the Latin text edited by Bensley:—"And behold, from the sea a great wind arose and stirred up all its waves. And I looked, and behold that wind caused to ascend from the heart of the sea as it were the likeness of a man. I looked, and behold this man flew with the clouds of heaven. And whithersoever he turned his face and gazed, there all things trembled when they were seen by him. And whithersoever the voice went forth out of his mouth, there all that heard his voice melted away as wax melts when it feels the fire. And after these things I looked, and behold a multitude of men that could not be numbered, were gathered together from the four winds of heaven, in order to come against the man who had ascended out of the sea. And I looked, and behold he hewed out for himself a great mountain, and flew upon it. But I sought to discover the region or the locality out of which the mountain had been hewn, but I could not. And after this I looked, and behold, all they that were gathered together against him in order to fight against him, were greatly afraid; nevertheless they dared to fight. And behold, when he observed the onslaught of the approaching multitude, he raised not his hand, nor did he clutch his sword, nor any other warlike weapon; I only saw how that he sent forth out of his mouth as it were a fiery stream, and from his lips flaming breath; and from his tongue there came out a storm of sparks; these were all mixed up together, the fiery stream, the flaming breath and the overwhelming storm. And these struck against the approaching multitude which had prepared to fight, and burned the whole of it, so that suddenly nothing was seen of the miserable multitude but the dust of ashes and the smell of smoke. And when I saw this I was terrified. And after this I saw that man descending from the mountain and calling unto him another, a peaceful multitude. And there were nigh unto him the figures of many men, some of them joyful, others sad; some of them bound, others led those whom they brought as offerings." In this passage there are a number of *traits* which are very much older than the book in which they have been embodied,[1] but

[1] See further on this, *The Messianic Teaching of iv. Esdras* in "The International Journal of Apocrypha," pp. 11ff. (Jan. 1908).

the Vision purports to describe the Advent of the Messiah, the annihilation of his enemies, *i.e.*, the wicked, and the blessedness of his followers, *i.e.*, the good; the Messianic reign of peace is then to be inaugurated. The interpretation of the Vision, as given in verses 21ff. of the same chapter, should also be read.

§iii. *The Judgement on the Wicked.*

This subject plays a very prominent part in the Old Testament as well as in the later literature; but here it is, of course, only in connection with eschatological thought that it is to be considered. The passages in which mention is made of the final lot of the Wicked are many in number in *Eth. Enoch*; only a small selection need be cited. In i. 9, we read: "And lo! He comes with ten thousands of His holy ones to execute judgement upon them, and He will destroy the ungodly, and will convict all flesh of all that the sinners and ungodly have wrought and ungodly committed against Him;" and so in many other passages. The place in which the Wicked are to suffer punishment is also mentioned; it is said in x. 12-14: "When all their sons have slain one another, and they have seen the destruction of their beloved ones, bind them fast under the hills of the earth for seventy generations, till the day of their judgement and of their consummation, till the judgement which is for ever and ever is consummated. In those days they will be led off to the abyss of fire; in torment and in prison will they be confined for ever and ever . . . ;" these are the words of the Lord spoken to Michael the Archangel. (See also xxii. 1-13; xvii. 1-5.) In lxiii. 10 (from the portion of this book known as *The Book of Celestial Physics*) the Wicked speak of their own punishment in these words: "Our souls are satisfied with the mammon of unrighteousness, but this does not prevent us from descending into the flame of the pain of Sheol." In *The Book of Similitudes* there are likewise frequent references to the doom of the Wicked (see xli. 1, 2.; xlv. 6; xlviii. 8-10; lvi. 8; lxii. 2; lxix. 27, 28). Passages dealing with the subject from other books of this class of literature are the following (only one example from each book is given): *The Sibylline Oracles* iii. 689ff.: "And God shall judge all men with war and sword, and fire, and overflowing rain, and brimstone shall descend from heaven . . . mourning and the cry of battle will be over the whole earth, when men will perish, and cascades will run with blood, yea, the earth herself will drink of the blood of those that perish." In speaking of the "seven heavens" it says in *The Testaments of the Twelve Patriarchs*, Levi iii. 2: "The second has fire, snow, ice ready for the day of the ordinance of the Lord in the righteous judgement of God. In it are all the spirits of the retributions for vengeance on the lawless." With this *cf.* Sir. xxxix. 28-30; xl. 9, 10. In *The Psalms of Solomon* xv. 12, 13, we read: "And in the Lord's Day of Judgement the sinners shall be destroyed for ever, when God will punish the earth with His judgement: . . . the sinners will go into everlasting destruction." So, too, in *The Book of Jubilees* xxxvi. 10, 11: "And in the day of confusion and curse and of wrath and indignation will He (God) burn, in the fire that burns and destroys, his (*i.e.* the wicked) land and his city and all that is his, like as He (God) burned Sodom; and he (*i.e.* the wicked man) shall be blotted out of the book of remembrance[1] of the children of men, and shall not be written in the book of life,[2] but in that of those who are destined to destruction; and he shall

[1] *Cf.* Mal. iii. 16.
[2] *Cf.* Ps. lxix. 28.

go to the eternal curse, in order that their judgement may be daily renewed for ever in shame and in perdition and in wrath, and in sorrow and in sickness." In *Slav. Enoch* x. 1-6 a vivid description is given of the place where the Wicked are to dwell eternally; after enumerating the various kinds of sinners, it says: "For all these this place is prepared for an eternal inheritance." (*Cf.* vii. 1ff.; lxi. 6ff.) A very curious conception is contained in *The Ascension of Isaiah* iv. 18, according to which the final punishment of the Wicked will not consist in torment, but in an annihilation resulting in absolute non-existence; this idea is contained in a passage from *The Testament of Hezekiah*, incorporated into this book: ". . . . And the Beloved will cause fire to go forth from Him, and it will consume all the godless, and they will be as though they had not been created." Once more, in *The Assumption of Moses* x. 3, we read: "For the Heavenly One will rise up from His throne, and will come forth from His holy dwelling-place[1] in indignation and in wrath because of His children." The whole passage needs to be read in order to realise to the full its eschatological character. Then we have in the Syriac

[1] *Cf.* Mic. i. 3.

Apocalypse of Baruch xxx. 4, 5, these words: "But the souls of the godless, when they shall see all this, will perish for fear; for they shall know that (the time of) their torment has come upon them, and that their destruction is at hand." (See also xliv. 15, and the whole of li.) Lastly, in *iv. Esdras* vi. 18-20, we read: "Behold, days are coming in the which I will come near to punish the inhabitants of the earth, when I shall come to make inqusition concerning the iniquity of the evil doers. . . ." (See also xi. 37, 38.)

On comparing the ideas on this subject with those contained in the Old Testament, the process of development will be sufficiently obvious.

§iv. *The Blessedness of the Righteous.*

This subject, like the preceding, occupies a very prominent place in the literature we are considering; it will be sufficient here, too, to give a single example from each work in order to show how uniform the teaching on the subject is. *Eth. Enoch* i. 8: "But to the righteous He will give peace, and He will protect the elect, and grace will be upon them, and they will all belong to God, and it will be well with them, and they will be blessed, and the light of God will shine upon them." (See, too, xcix. 10ff.; c. 5; cii. 4; ciii. 1ff.) In *The Book of Similitudes* lxii. 13-16, we read: "And the righteous and elect will be saved on that day . . . and there shall be your garments, garments of life, before the Lord of Spirits; and your garments will not grow old, and your glory will not pass away before the Lord of Spirits." (See, too, xli. 1, 2; xlv. 4; l. 1; lviii. 3-6; lxix. 26.) *Sibylline Oracles* iii. 580-582: "In righteousness and in joy shall they inherit the cities and the fruitful fields, for they have attained to the Law of the Most High. They shall become prophets themselves, raised up by the Immortal One, and shall bring great joy to all men."[1] (See, further, verses 702-731, 767-784.) *The Testaments of the Twelve Patriarchs*, Levi xviii. 12, 13: "And Beliar shall be bound by Him, and He shall give power to His children to tread upon the evil spirits. And the Lord shall rejoice in His children, and be well pleased in His beloved ones for ever." (See also Judah xxv. 3-5; Dan. v. 12, 13.) *The Psalms of Solomon* xv. 13: "But they who fear the Lord shall then find mercy and shall live in the grace of their God" (*cf.* xviii. 6-9). *The Book of Jubilees* xxiii. 29: "And all their days shall they fulfil in peace

[1] *Cf.* Dan. xii. 3.

and joy, and they shall live, for there will be no Satan and no Evil One to destroy them, but all their days will be days of blessing and salvation;" the succeeding verses are to the same effect. *Slav. Enoch* lxv. 8: "There shall be one eternity, and all the just who shall escape the great judgement of the Lord shall be gathered together in eternal life, and for ever and ever the just shall be gathered together, and they shall be eternal." (See also lxi. 1ff.; lxvi. 7.) *The Ascension of Isaiah* (*The Testament of Hezekiah*) iv. 15-17: "And He will give rest to the godly whom He shall find in the body in this world. . . . But the saints will come with the Lord[1] with their garments which are stored up on high in the seventh heaven; with the Lord will they come, whose spirits are clothed, they will descend and be present in the world, and He will strengthen those that have been found in the body, together with the saints, in the garments of the saints,[2] and the Lord will minister to those who have kept watch in this world."[3] *The Assumption of Moses* x. i: "And then shall appear his rule over all creatures; then shall the devil come to an end, and with him sorrow shall be taken

[1] *Cf.* 1 Thess. iii. 13; 2 Thess. i. 10.
[2] *Cf.* Luke xxiv. 4. [3] *Cf.* 1 Thess. v. 6; Rev. xvi. 15.

away" (*cf.* verses 8-10). The Syriac *Apocalypse of Baruch* has many passages of a similar kind, *e.g.*, li. 7-12: " . . . . For they shall dwell in the high places of that world, and they shall be like the angels[1] and shall be comparable with the stars. . . . And then shall the glory of the righteous be greater than that of the angels. . . ." (See, further, xxix. 6-8, xliv. 13-15, and the beautiful passage lxxiii. 1-7.) Finally, *iv. Esdras* vi. 25-28: "And whosoever remaineth after all these things that I foretold to thee, shall be saved and shall see my salvation, and shall behold the end of my world. Then shall appear the men who were aforetime taken up and who have not tasted of death since their birth; then shall the heart of those who inhabit the earth be turned and be changed to a new spirit.[2] . . ." (See also xiii. 39-40.) By those who "have not tasted death" are meant Enoch and Elijah, and possibly Moses, in view of the words in Deut. xxxvi. 6: *No man knoweth of his sepulchre unto this day;* as regards Enoch, see *Slav. Enoch* ii. 4: "And now, my children, let no one seek me till the Lord brings me back to you."

[1] *Cf.* Luke xx. 36: *For they are equal to the angels; and are sons of God, being sons of the resurrection.*
[2] *Cf.* Ezek. xxxvi. 26.

CHAPTER VI.

SOME FURTHER ESCHATOLOGICAL ELEMENTS IN THE APOCALYPTIC LITERATURE.

In chap. iii. we referred briefly to some points of subsidiary importance belonging to the Eschatological Drama. The first of these, namely *Theophanies*, was mentioned because the details of the later eschatological conceptions are apparently based upon much that we read in the Old Testament concerning divine appearances. This fact lies in the natural order of things; for the Apocalyptists, in creating their mental pictures of what was to take place in the "last times," were necessarily very much influenced by what they had read and studied in the Scriptures. But in the Apocalyptic literature there is only one Theophany which is spoken of, that of the "last times"; there is nothing parallel to the other divine appearances which are described in the Old Testament; nevertheless, the conceptions concerning the final great Theophany, as contained in the Apocalyptic literature, are based upon, and receive their colouring, in the main, from the various Theophanic descriptions of the Old Testament; this subject, as far as the Apocalyptic literature is concerned, has been dealt with in §§i. ii. of the preceding chapter, and need not be further treated here. But the other matters spoken of in chap. iii. require some further attention here, as they recur in the Apocalyptic writings.

§i. *The Gathering of the Gentiles.*

We saw, in dealing with the Old Testament presentation of this subject, that two entirely different attitudes were taken up with regard to the Gentiles; there was the *Particularist* attitude, which, in its narrow nationalism, regarded all non-Jews as outside the pale of divine recognition, and which saw in the gathering of the Gentiles in the "last times" the great occasion for their final destruction. On the other hand, there was the *Universalist* attitude, which, in its wider outlook upon the world, taught that the divine mercy was not restricted in its action to the Jewish nation, but that the Gentile world would also be embraced in the number of those who would be accepted by God, and that therefore in the "last times" the gathering of the Gentiles would take place in order that their salvation, too, might be proclaimed. These two attitudes also figure in the Apocalyptic literature. The different works incorporated into *The Ethiopic Book of Enoch* are almost wholly Universalistic in character;[1] the two great divisions of mankind are not Jew and Gentile, but the righteous and the sinners, the differentiation between Jew and Gentile scarcely ever occurs in the eschatological portions, a notable exception to this, however, will be noted presently. To give one or two illustrations of this, in xci. 14 we read: "And after that, in the ninth week, the righteous judgement will be revealed to the whole world, and all the works of the godless will vanish from the whole earth, and the world will be written down for destruction, and all mankind will look to the path of uprightness." Likewise in *The Book of Similitudes* xxxviii. 2: "And when the Righteous One shall appear before the eyes of

[1] *The Book of Celestial Physics* does not come into consideration here.

the elect righteous whose works are wrought in dependence on the Lord of Spirits, and light will appear to the righteous and the elect who dwell on the earth—where then will be the dwelling of the sinners, and where the resting-place of those who have denied the Lord of Spirits? It had been good for them if they had not been born." Still more pointed is xlviii. 4, 5: "He will be a staff to the righteous on which they will support themselves and not fall, and He will be the light of the Gentiles[1] and the hope of those who are troubled of heart. All who dwell on the earth will fall down and bow the knee before Him, and will bless and laud and celebrate with song the Lord of Spirits." A feature which occurs both in the Old Testament and in the Apocalyptic literature is that the wicked will in the final issue be delivered into the hand of the righteous, in order, presumably, that these may take their vengeance on the former; see, *e.g.*, *Eth. Enoch* xci.: "And after that there will be another week, the eighth, that of righteousness, and a sword will be given to it that judgement and righteousness may be executed on those who commit oppression, and sinners will be delivered into

[1] *Cf.* Luke ii. 32.

the hands of the righteous." An instance of the superiority of Israel over the Gentiles, the only one in the book,[1] is found in l. 2-5: "And on the day of affliction, evil will gather over the sinners, but the righteous will be victorious in the name of the Lord of Spirits: and He will cause the Gentiles (literally 'the others') to witness (this judgement) that they may repent and forego the works of their hands. They will have no honour through the name of the Lord of Spirits, yet through His name will they be saved, and the Lord of Spirits will have compassion on them, for His compassion is great. And He is righteous in His judgement, and in the presence of His glory and in His judgement no unrighteousness shall maintain itself; whosoever repents not before Him will perish. And from henceforth He will show no mercy to them, saith the Lord of Spirits." As pointed out by Professor Charles in commenting on this passage, the Gentiles who repent will be saved as by fire; they will not have the abundant entering in of the Jews; when once the Judgement arrives the lot of the Gentiles is finally fixed. In *The Sibylline Oracles* the spirit is, upon the whole,

[1] Charles shows, however, that this passage is an interpolation, see his edition, pp. 138ff.

Universalistic, but the superiority of Israel is sometimes distinctly asserted, as, *e.g.*, in iii. 194ff.: "And then shall the people of the great God become strong again, and they shall direct into the way of life (literally 'they shall be the sign-post of life to') all those who are mortal." The Universalistic spirit, again, is still more strongly marked in *The Testaments of the Twelve Patriarchs*; in Levi xviii. (the whole chapter is eschatological) verse 9, we read: "And in his (*i.e.*, the Messiah's) priesthood the Gentiles shall be multiplied in knowledge upon the earth, and enlightened through the grace of the Lord . . . ;" again in Naph. viii. 3: "For through their tribes shall God appear on earth, to save the race of Israel, and to gather together the righteous from among the Gentiles." In the following verse, however, the superiority of the Israelites seems to be implied, for it continues: "If ye work that which is good, my children, both men and angels shall bless you; and God shall be glorified among the Gentiles through you . . . ;" but the normal attitude of this book towards the Gentiles and their lot in the "last times" is unquestionably reflected in such a passage as Asher vii. 3: "Until the Most High shall visit the earth, coming Himself

. . . He shall save Israel and all the Gentiles." (*Cf.* Benj. ix. 2.) In *The Assumption of Moses* this subject is only slightly touched upon; a Particularist attitude is revealed in x. 7: "For the Most High God, Who alone is eternal, shall arise and shall come forth manifestly in order to punish the Gentiles and to destroy all their idols." The verses which follow speak of the glorification of Israel, see the next section on this. In the Syriac *Apocalypse of Baruch* it is taught that the gathering of the Gentiles in the "last times" is in the main for their destruction, those who are saved will owe their salvation to the fact of their not having been the enemies of Israel. In lxxii. 2ff., for example, it says: "After the signs of which thou hast already been told—when the Gentiles shall be thrown into confusion, and the time of my Messiah shall have come—then shall He call for all the Gentiles, and some He shall preserve alive and some He shall destroy. This is therefore what shall come from Him upon the Gentiles who shall be preserved alive: every people that has not known Israel and has not down-trodden the family of Jacob, this shall be preserved alive . . . but all those who have set themselves over you or have otherwise known you, these all shall be delivered over to the sword." As regards *iv. Esdras*, the teaching of this book on the subject will already have been gathered from the long extract given in §ii. of the preceding chapter, to which reference should be made. (See also *iv. Esdras* vii. 33ff.) On the whole, therefore, the feeling of the Apocalyptic writers seems to have been that some non-Israelitish nations would be saved in the "last times," and that their being gathered together in "that Day" would not be wholly for destruction. The best Apocalyptic works and those which most probably reflect in the truest way the normal attitude of the Apocalyptic Movement in this particular respect, such as *The Book of Enoch* and *The Testaments of the Twelve Patriarchs*, are frankly Universalistic, and in them is adumbrated the Gospel teaching on this point.

§ii. *The Ingathering of Israel.*

One of the main ideas which come to the fore in connection with this subject is that the Israelites scattered all over the world are to be brought together to the Holy Land for the purpose of enjoying the time of bliss which is to follow the signs of the "last times": but, as will have been seen in the preceding section, the Apocalyptic writers realise that the fact of being an Israelite is not in itself sufficient to save him from the divine wrath in the "last times" if in other respects he is not worthy to be a partaker of the bliss to come; and therefore they divide men into the *righteous* and the *wicked*, not into *Israel* and the *Gentiles*; and the object, then, of the ingathering of Israel is that they should be differentiated, the faithful being destined to life, the wicked to destruction. It is worth while recalling in this connection the words of the Baptist in Luke iii. 7ff. . . . *Ye offspring of vipers, who warned you to flee from the wrath to come? Bring forth therefore fruits worthy of repentance, and begin not to say within yourselves, We have Abraham to our father; for I say unto you that God is able of these stones to raise up children unto Abraham.* . . . This thought is, without doubt, based upon the prophetic teaching of the need of national purification; only the righteous, even among those of the seed of Israel, may look forward to happiness when the "last times" are past. But a further thought, already noticed in passing in the preceding section, in connection with this subject is that the ingathering of Israel is to serve as a means whereby the righteous among the Gentiles may also be brought in. This, as we have seen, is also to be traced to prophetic influence; and it reveals an intermediate position between the Particularist and Universalist attitudes. These three thoughts must now be briefly illustrated. It will be obvious that the first thought referred to—that of the ingathering of Israel for the purpose of insuring their bliss after the "last times," without a consideration of their worthiness but simply because they are of the seed of Abraham—is not one that we should expect to find prominently expressed in the Apocalyptic literature; it came to the fore in somewhat later times, as we shall see in the next chapter; but the Apocalyptists were too Universalistic and too much influenced by the spirit of the prophets to express this thought unconditionally. Perhaps the pious writer of the ninth psalm in *The Psalms of Solomon* comes nearest to it, but the passage to be cited is preceded by words which show the writer's conviction that repentance is indispensable to those who would have final recognition from God: "And now, Thou art God, and we are the nation that Thou lovest; look upon us and have mercy, oh God of Israel, for we are thine, and turn not away Thy compassion from us, that they (*i.e.*, the Gentiles) may not overcome us. For Thou hast chosen the seed of Abraham above all nations, and hast laid Thy name upon us, oh Lord, and wilt not cast us off for ever. Thou didst make a covenant with our fathers for our sakes, and we hope in Thee that Thou wilt grant peace to our heart. The mercy of the Lord shall be upon the house of Israel for ever and ever" (ix. 8-11). This passage, it is true, is not strictly eschatological, but it displays a spirit which is inclined to regard the Israelites as the recipients of eternal mercy just because they are of the seed of Abraham; but Psalms xi., xvii., and xviii. of the book should also be consulted. The thought of the destruction of wicked Israelites in the "last times" and the salvation of the upright finds expression in *The Testaments of the Twelve Patriarchs*, Benj. ix. 1: "And I believe that there will be also evil-doings among you, from the words of Enoch the righteous; that ye shall commit fornication with the fornication of Sodom, and shall perish, all save a few, and shall renew wanton deeds with women; and the Kingdom of the Lord shall not be among you, for straightway He shall take it away." The purification of Israel preparatory to their inheriting the Kingdom is spoken of, for example, in the same book, Asher vii. 5-7: "For I have known that ye shall assuredly be disobedient, and assuredly act ungodly, not giving heed to the law of God, but to the commandments of men, being corrupted through wickedness. And therefore shall ye be scattered as Gad and Dan, my brethren, and ye shall know not your own lords, tribe and tongue. But the Lord will gather you together in faith through His tender mercy, and for the sake of Abraham, Isaac and Jacob."[1] For an example illustrating the thought that Israel is to be the means whereby in the last day others shall be saved, see *Sibylline Oracles* iii. 194ff. quoted in §i. of this chapter,[2] and *cf.* *Eth. Enoch* xc. 30.

§iii. *The Resurrection of the Dead.*

The beginnings of the belief in this doctrine are to be sought in the Old Testament (see chap. iii. §iv.), but we find it greatly developed

[1] This passage belongs, according to Charles, to the first century B.C.
[2] Page 110.

in the Apocalyptic literature; the fact that it forms an integral part of eschatological teaching is the reason of its mention here. According to the older view the Messianic Kingdom, *i.e.*, the time of bliss which follows the "last times," was to come after the Resurrection and the Judgement; but the later and more widely held view was that a temporary Messianic Kingdom would be established on the earth which would be followed by the Last Judgement and the Resurrection. The Messiah Himself was to judge the nations, who, together with their guardian-angels and stars, are destined to be cast into Gehenna.

In later times belief in a universal Resurrection became prevalent (see below, chap. vii. §v.). In illustrating this belief in the Apocalyptic literature we turn, as usual, first to *Eth. Enoch*; in the rather difficult ninetieth chapter a general resurrection, including Gentiles as well as Israelites, seems to be implied in verse 33, where it says: "And all that had been destroyed and dispersed, and all the beasts of the field, and all the birds of the heaven assembled in that house, and the Lord of the sheep rejoiced with great joy because they were all good and had returned to His house." According to xci. 10 it is only the righteous who attain to the Resurrection: "And the righteous one (used collectively) shall arise from the sleep (*i.e.*, of death), and Wisdom will rise up and will be accorded to them." In xlii. 1 it is said that Wisdom had before withdrawn to the heavens because there was no place on earth where she could dwell. In *The Book of Similitudes* there is some uncertainty as to whether the Resurrection is to be a general one, or whether it is only the righteous who shall attain to it; thus in li. 1, 2, the reference is to a general Resurrection, but only the righteous are chosen for eternal life, the wicked are personally destined for eternal punishment: "And in those days will the earth also give back those who are treasured up within it, and Sheol also will give back that which it has received, and Hell will give back that which it owes.[1] And He will choose the righteous and holy from among them; for the day of their redemption has drawn nigh" (*cf.* lxi. 5). Professor Charles holds that the resurrection here is a resurrection of all Israel, but not of the Gentiles, because no Jewish book before *iv. Esdras* teaches *indubitably* the doctrine of

[1] *Cf.* Rev. xx. 13.

a general resurrection; the whole history of Jewish thought points to a restricted belief in this matter. In *The Testaments of the Twelve Patriarchs* it is a belief in the resurrection of the righteous in Israel that is taught; thus we read in Simeon vi. 7: "Then shall I arise in joy, and will bless the Most High because of His marvellous works" (see the whole passage). See also Judah xxv. 1; Zeb. x. 2; but in Benj. x. 6-8, on the other hand, we have this remarkable passage: "Then shall ye see Enoch, Noah, and Shem, and Abraham, and Isaac, and Jacob, rising on the right hand in gladness. Then shall we also rise, each one over our tribe, worshipping the King of heaven. Then also all men shall rise, some unto glory and some unto shame. And the Lord shall judge Israel first, for their uprighteousness. And then shall He judge all the Gentiles. . . ."[1] It is to be noted that the wicked as well as the righteous rise, according to this passage; that is a considerable development upon earlier teaching. In *Slav. Enoch* there does not appear to be any direct reference to a resurrection, but apparently it is to be implied in those passages in which a blessed immortality

[1] The interpolations are omitted, *see* Charles's edition.

of the just is referred to, *e.g.*, i. 2: "Now, therefore, my children, in patience and meekness accomplish the number of your days, and ye shall inherit the endless life which is to come." (*Cf.* xxii. 8; lxv. 6ff.) A very interesting passage is lxi. 2, 3: "For in the world to come, I know all things, how that there are many mansions prepared for men. . . . Blessed are all those who shall go to the mansions of the blessed." One is irresistibly reminded of the words in John xiv. 2: *In my Father's house are many mansions; if it were not so I would have told you; for I go to prepare a place for you.*

At the same time it must be said that this book offers very little of a specifically eschatological character.

In *The Psalms of Solomon* the Resurrection of the righteous in Israel at the last day is plainly taught, *e.g.*, iii. 12: "But they that fear the Lord shall arise unto eternal life; their life shall be in light, and it will never cease" (*cf.* xiii. 11; xiv. 3). In the Syriac *Apocalypse of Baruch* the Resurrection is referred to several times, *e.g.*, xxx. 1: "And after that, when the time of the Advent of the Messiah is completed, he shall return in glory into the heavens. And then shall all those arise who slept having their hope in him" (*cf.* xlii. 7; xlix. 1-3). Lastly, we turn to *iv. Esdras*, but here it must be remembered that the possibility of Christian influence regarding this subject has to be reckoned with. In vii. 32, 33, we read: "The earth gives up again they that rest in her, the dust returns them that sleep in her, the chambers deliver up the souls that were committed unto them. The Most High appears upon the Judgement-seat . . . ;" it is clear that a universal Resurrection of all mankind is here referred to. (*Cf.* also viii. 53, 54.)

It will thus be seen that there are two tendencies in the Apocalyptic literature regarding a belief in the Resurrection; sometimes it seems to be restricted to Israel, at other times a wider view is taken, and all mankind is embraced; then again, sometimes it is taught that the righteous only rise from the dead, and at other times that the good and the bad rise, the former entering into eternal life, the latter into eternal death. It is, however, scarcely necessary to emphasise the fact that this belief falls short of the Christian doctrine of the Resurrection of the body.

§iv. *The Messianic Banquet.*

Whatever may have been the origin of this idea, it may be regarded as very probable that it received an *impetus* in course of time from the holding of kingly banquets; Jewish conceptions regarding the Messianic Era were to a large extent materialistic, based in many particulars upon what men saw to be in vogue among earthly rulers; this was very natural, for, after all, the Jewish belief in a Messiah pictured him as a temporal sovereign, generally speaking, and his Kingdom was conceived of as an earthly one, though more perfect than any other could ever be. In accordance, therefore, with these materialistic ideas was the belief that the Messianic ruler would furnish a Banquet for his people. This Banquet is referred to in *Eth. Enoch* (*The Book of Similitudes*) lxii. 14: "And the Lord of Spirits will abide over them, and with that Son of Man will they eat and lie down and rise up for ever and ever." (See also xxv. 4, 5.) Possibly a reference is also contained to it in *The Testaments of the Twelve Patriarchs*, Levi xviii. 11: "And He shall give to the saints to eat from the tree of life;" but judging from the later Jewish teaching on the subject (see below, chap. vii.) it was the carcase of Leviathan which was to be consumed at the Messianic Banquet. The most detailed account of this Banquet in the Apocalyptic literature is contained in the Syriac *Apocalypse of Baruch* xxix. 3-8, where it says: ". . . . Then will the Messiah begin to manifest Himself. And Behemoth will show himself from his land, and Leviathan will ascend from the sea; and these two mighty sea-monsters, whom I created on the fifth day of the work of Creation and have reserved until that time (*i.e.*, the Messianic Era), shall then be for food for all those who are left." The following verses then go on to describe the fruitfulness of the earth and the abundance of food which shall be brought forth in order that they who have hungered may hunger no more. In this connection *Eth. Enoch* lx. 7, 8, is of interest: "And on that day will two monsters be parted, a female monster named Leviathan, to dwell in the depths of the ocean over the fountains of the waters. But the whale is called Behemoth, who occupies with his breast a waste wilderness named Dêndâin, on the east of the garden where the elect and righteous dwell."

See also *Sibylline Oracles*, Procem. 87, iii. 746; and *iv. Esdras* vi. 49-52: "Then didst Thou preserve two living creatures, the one Thou calledst Behemoth, and the other Thou calledst Leviathan . . . . and Thou hast kept them to be devoured of whom Thou wilt and when." In each of these passages the thought of the Messianic Banquet is probably present.

SUMMARY OF THE TEACHING IN THE APOCALYPTIC LITERATURE.

It will have been seen that the Apocalyptic literature continues, and in some respects develops, the eschatological teaching of the Old Testament. Thus the signs which precede the end are described very much in the same way as in the prophetical books; there is more fulness of detail in the later literature, and not infrequently the descriptions become somewhat fantastic and exaggerated; but in the main points the teaching of the two classes of literature is identical—the terrifying physical phenomena, darkness on the earth and awful portents in the sun, moon and stars, great terror among men, wars among the nations, the nearest ties of relationship broken by strife and murder. Then, again, we find a striking similarity of teaching in the fact that the central figure in the Eschatological Drama is sometimes stated to be God Himself, at other times the Messiah, who, in *The Book of Enoch*, is often spoken of as the Son of Man; the expression "the throne of His glory" is often used in the same book in connection with the Advent. Jerusalem is to be the centre of the new Kingdom which is to be founded,[1] though this is not always stated, any more than it is in the Old Testament accounts. Thirdly, the punishment of the Wicked in that day is often described, and here again with more detail than in the Old Testament; it is also noteworthy that as regards this point the Apocalyptic literature is, as a rule, more general; that is to say, the Universalistic attitude is, upon the whole, more pronounced. The same applies to the fourth point, namely, the blessedness of the Righteous; although Israel is often singled out as the people of Jehovah for whom the Kingdom is to be prepared, yet, for the most part, it is taught that righteous men, irrespective of race, will enjoy the happiness of the Hereafter. The idea of the forerunner also finds expres-

[1] On this point see further below, chap. x.

sion here. As in the Old Testament so in this later literature present historical conditions are frequently used as the basis of eschatological teaching. Then, as regards the subsidiary points, the various descriptions of the gathering of the Gentiles exhibit precisely the same marks as in the Old Testament, though, upon the whole, the Particularistic attitude, with some exceptions, is less marked in this later literature; we also find the feature that the Israelite nation is to be the medium of salvation for the Gentiles; but as in the Old Testament, so here, the gathering of the Gentiles is sometimes described as about to take place in order that they may be destroyed by Jehovah, or His army, and that the Israelites may rejoice over their discomfiture; these varying standpoints are partly conditioned by historical circumstances, and partly by the two tendencies already referred to. The subject of the Ingathering of Israel is treated in very much the same way as in the Old Testament, excepting that, upon the whole, the Universalistic attitude predominates. The belief in the Resurrection is greatly developed in the Apocalyptic literature, though the teaching as to when it is to take place, whether before or after the establishment of the Messianic

Kingdom, is not uniform ; in like manner, there is a difference of view as to whether there is to be a general Resurrection, *i.e.*, of both good and bad, or whether it is to be restricted to the former ; also as to whether it is to be for all men or for the Israelites only. The details about the Messianic Banquet are, as we should rather expect, given much more fully here than in the Old Testament.

It will thus be seen that in essentials the eschatological teaching of the Apocalyptic literature is in entire agreement with that of the Old Testament, the differences being almost entirely due to the fact that development has taken place in the later writings.

CHAPTER VII.

ESCHATOLOGICAL TEACHING IN RABBINICAL LITERATURE.

It may not be altogether without interest, as illustrating the growth of some of the ideas referred to in the preceding chapters, to take a brief glance at some of the eschatological ideas contained in the later Jewish literature. Frequently, however, what is said on the subject in this literature reflects much earlier thought; so that while in some cases we may trace development, in others it is nothing more than the crystallisation of traditions that have been handed down for generations.

§i. *The Signs which precede the End.*[1]

In Rabbinical writings the technical term for the terrors of the "last times," previous

[1] These sections should be compared with the corresponding ones in chaps. ii., iii., v., vi.

to the Advent of the Messiah, is *Cheble ha-Meshiach* or *Cheblo shel Mashiach*, the "birth-pangs,"[1] or "travail" of the Messiah (*Shabbath* 118*a*). In the Mishnah tractate, *Sota* ix. 15, we have the following account of these travails: "As traces of the approach of Messiah are to be regarded that arrogance increases, ambition shoots up, that the vine yields fruit and yet wine is dear. The government turns to heresy. There is no instruction. The place of assembly (the synagogue) is devoted to lewdness. Galilee is destroyed, Gablan laid waste. The inhabitants of a district go from city to city without finding compassion. The wisdom of the learned is hated, the godly despised, truth is absent. Boys insult old men, old men stand in the presence of children. The son depreciates his father, the daughter rebels against the mother, the daughter-in-law against the mother-in-law. A man's enemies are his house-fellows."[2] In the "years" immediately preceding the Advent of the Messiah each year is to be characterised by a special plague; the rise of false Messiahs

[1] The meaning assigned to the expression "birth-pangs of the Messiah" is, perhaps, a later figurative adaptation of what was in the first place understood literally. It may be a survival of the myth wherein the birth of the Messiah of the "woman" was described (*cf.* Rev. xii. 1ff.; Oesterley and Box, *op. cit.* p. 218).

[2] See Schürer, *The Jewish People in the Time of Jesus Christ*, II. ii. p. 155.

is also one of the signs of the end; the study of the *Torah* ("Law") will cease, heresy will increase, and men will give up hoping for the Messiah[1] (*Sanhedrin* 97*a*); see also ***Pesikta* 51*b*.** In the *Apocalypse of Abraham* xxx., a Jewish work of the second century A.D., ten "plagues" are mentioned as portents of the Advent of the Messiah: distress, fire, pestilence among the beasts, famine, earthquakes, and wars, hail and frost, ravening wild beasts, pestilence and death among men, destruction and flight, and subterranean noises. The War of Gog and Magog is also frequently referred to in Rabbinical literature (***Berachoth*** 7*b*, ***Pesikta*** 79*a*, etc.; see, for further references, the *Jewish Encyclopædia*, v. 212; and §iii. of this chapter).

§ii. *The Advent of the Messiah.*

In Rabbinical literature there is never any ambiguity about the central person of the Eschatological Drama; in the Old Testament it is sometimes Jevohah Himself Whose Advent as Judge is looked for, at other times it is one who is subordinate to Him; in the Apocalyptic literature also we come across passages in which God Himself is the central

[1] A saying of Rabbi Simon ben Jochai.

figure at the "last times," though more generally it is His Messiah. In the writings which we are now considering it is invariably the Messiah, and none other, whose Advent is spoken of. But it is taught that the Advent of the Messiah is only an episode in the life of one who has existed from all time; King Messiah, it is said, pre-existed before the Creation of the world.[1] According to Weber, however, the meaning of this statement is that it was God's will from all eternity to create the Messiah and to send Him into the world;[2] that is to say, He existed potentially, but not actually, from all time. In the later Jewish theology it is taught that the Messiah lives in the Garden of Eden. But in spite of this pre-existence of the Messiah, whether from all eternity or of more limited duration, He is to be born of a woman and is to be of the seed of David (*Bereshith rabbah* c. xii., *Sanhedrin* 93*b*); it is said in *Pesikta* 149*a*: "Happy the hour in which the Messiah was born, happy the womb from which he came forth![3] Happy the generation that sees him; happy the eye that is honoured by looking up him!"[4] Thus the Messiah is always regarded

[1] *Cf.* John viii. 58.
[2] Weber, *Juedische Theologie*, p. 355ff.
[3] *Cf.* Luke xi. 27.
[4] Weber, *op. cit.* p. 355.

as *human* and nothing more, and this in spite of His being reckoned as superior to the angels. It is instructive to observe that the accounts of the actual Advent of the Messiah in Rabbinical literature are generally wanting in all the supernatural *traits* which we read of in the Old Testament descriptions of the Advent as well as in those of the Apocalyptic literature; this must in great part, if not altogether, be due to the purely human character ascribed to the Messiah in Rabbinical literature. He comes as the warring champion of His people to deliver them from the oppression of their enemies; this is clearly seen in the *Targum of Jonathan* to Isa. lii. 14, 15; it is here said that at the Messiah's Advent He will destroy many peoples, and He will silence Kings by His wonderful deeds; then, in dealing with Isa. liii. 2, the *Targum* tells of the coming Messiah as the Righteous One; and there follows a description of His power and majesty; He will annihilate the wealthy and the great, and thus take away the reproach of His people. As the deliverer (*Goel;* "Redeemer" seems too strong a word to use, as it connotes more in Christian phraseology than in Jewish) of His people, the Messiah is compared to Moses, who delivered the Israelites from the Egyptian bondage (*cf.* 1 Cor. x. 1-4); and it is said, therefore, that just as Moses lived in retirement before he came forth for his work of leading the Israelites out of Egypt, so will the Messiah be in hiding for some time previous to His Advent; this is brought out in *Pesikta* 49*b*: "Just as the first Goel (*i.e.*, Moses) manifested himself to Israel and then hid himself from them, so will the last Goel (*i.e.*, the Messiah) manifest himself first, and then hide himself from the people. For how long?—For forty-five days, according to Dan. xii. 11. 12. And whither will he lead them? Some say: into the Judæan desert; others: into the desert of Sihon and Og, according to Hos. ii. 16. . . . ."[1]

These passages are sufficient to show that the teaching in Rabbinical literature concerning the actual Advent differs considerably from that of the Old Testament and Apocalyptic literature.

§iii. *The Judgement on the Wicked.*

One of the main elements in Rabbinical Eschatology is the War of Gog and Magog (*cf.* chap. iii. §ii.); this idea is, of course,

[1] Weber, *op. cit.* p. 364.

based on Ezek. xxxviii. 14-xxxix. 16, but it is greatly elaborated in this later literature. This "War" represents the final attack of the Gentiles, expressed collectively by the term "Gog and Magog," upon the Messiah and His faithful followers; the point of the whole conception is to set forth the doctrine of the Judgement upon the Wicked in the "last times." As is to be expected, a Particularistic attitude is taken in the Rabbinical writings, that is to say, the Gentiles are as a body regarded as the "Wicked," and as such are to be condemned to eternal punishment, while the people of the Messiah, *i.e.*, the Jews, are to inherit the happiness and glory of the Messianic Kingdom. At the same time, it is only fair to remember that the Rabbis were to a large extent forced into this Particularistic attitude by their contemplation of the actual sinfulness of the non-Jewish world; above all, the non-recognition of Jehovah and the non-observance of His Law on the part of the Gentile world must have made the heathen peoples appear as outside the pale of divine mercy in the eyes of the Rabbis. This is well illustrated in *Abodah Zarah* 3*b*, where it is said that the War of Gog and Magog against the Messiah is not only undertaken because of the enmity of the Gentiles towards the Messiah, but also because they desire to do away altogether with the Law of God. Moreover, it is not only against the Law of God that the Gentiles are described as fighting in the "last times," but against God Himself; thus Rabbi Levi, in *Pesikta* 79*a*, explains the words of Zech. xiv. 3 (*Then shall the Lord go forth, and fight against those nations, as when he fought in the day of battle*) as referring to the "last times," and God is made to say to the Gentiles: "Sinner, thou comest to try conclusions with Me! As thou livest, I will make war against thee."[1] In the same way in *Mechilta* 48*b*, Psalm ii. is explained as referring to the War of Gog and Magog; Jehovah laughs them to scorn, the armies of Gog and Magog will suffer the fate of Pharaoh and his host, they will be swallowed up by the deep, so that the very fish will tremble (*cf.* Ezek. xxxviii. 20); it is Jehovah Himself Who will fight against Gog and Magog, and will destroy the Gentile hosts, Israel alone will be saved.[2] (See, further, the next section.)

Speaking generally, therefore, the Judge-

[1] Weber, *op. cit.* p. 389.
[2] *Ibid.*

ment on the Wicked in the "last times" is to be executed, according to Rabbinical teaching, rather on account of Gentile *enmity* than on account of their wickedness; though they are reckoned among the wicked indiscriminately because of their repudiation of the Law of Jehovah. (See, further, the *Targum of Pseudo-Jonathan* on Num. xi. 26.)

§iv. *The Blessedness of the Righteous.*

From what has been said in the preceding section we shall expect to find Particularistic views held with regard to the Righteous in Rabbinical literature; and for the most part this is so. It is Israel, the people of the Law, for whom Blessedness is reserved. The materialistic views always held with regard to the Messianic Kingdom naturally resulted in the idea, not infrequently expressed, that in the Messianic Era the requirements of the Law—in particular the sacrificial and priestly laws—would be strictly observed; it was this observance which constituted righteousness, and brought with it its reward. It is true that sometimes another and very remarkable view is met with, viz., that a new Law would be proclaimed by the Messiah; in the *Targum* to Isa. xii. 3, for example, it says: "Ye shall receive a new Law from the Elect One of the Righteous"; and a Midrashic passage, commenting on Eccles. xi. 8. (*All is vanity*), declares: "The Law which man learns in this world is nothing in comparison with the Law of the Messiah" (*Midrash Koheleth*, on xi. 8). But the Righteous who are to enjoy this Law are the Chosen People, and they only. The general attitude of Rabbinical teaching on this subject is expressed in the *Talmud* thus: "In the Messianic time no proselytes will be received" (*Abodah Zarah* 3*b*). But within the ranks of Israel a great differentiation is made between the righteous and the evil, and their lot in the "last times" is very different. The wicked Israelites share the same fate as the heathen Gentiles; they are to die the eternal death in Gehenna; this is their merited punishment. This teaching is, however, often found modified; it is taught that originally Gehenna was never intended to receive Israelites, but only Gentiles; but, at any rate, for Israelites it is only a place of purification, while for the Gentiles it is a place of punishment. Then, again, it is taught that Gehenna is only for those Gentiles who have forsaken God and served idols

(*Sanhedrin* 105*a*), so that here the blessedness of the Righteous among the Gentiles is contemplated. Later Judaism takes this milder and more rational view.[1] Of the lot of the Righteous and the Wicked, generally, after the "last times," the few following references will give a good idea: in *Abodah Zarah* 3*b* it is said of the sun that with its blazing rays it will torment the Wicked, but refresh the Righteous; in *Shemoth rabbah* c. xiv. it is said that in Gehenna the Wicked are covered in darkness; in *Bereshith rabbah* c. xii. it is said that death shall be altogether taken away; this must, of course, be spoken of in reference to the Righteous; above all things, after the terrors of the "last times" have passed away, the Righteous who will have been spared will enjoy great peace in the Messianic Kingdom.

From the two preceding sections it will be seen that the Judgement upon the Wicked and the Blessedness of the Righteous include the subjects of the Gathering of the Gentiles and the Ingathering of Israel; for the final gathering together of these is, speaking quite generally, for the purpose of assigning to them their punishment and reward respectively. It will, therefore, not be necessary to devote

[1] Weber, *op. cit.* pp. 390ff.

special sections here to the consideration of their final gathering. (See chaps. iii. §§ii., iii.; vi. §§i. ii.)

§v. *The Resurrection of the Dead.*

As we have already seen (chaps. iii. §iv.; vi. §iii.), the Resurrection formed part of the Messianic hope both in Old Testament and Apocalyptic writings. The Rabbinical literature has much to say on this subject; in the first place, "the very term used to express the idea of sharing in the future life is 'to inherit the land' (*Sanhedrin* xi. 1, with reference to Isa. lx. 21). The Resurrection, therefore, was believed to take place solely in the Holy Land (*Pesikta rabbah* i. after Psalm cxvi. 9). . . . Jerusalem alone is the city of which the dead shall blossom forth like grass (*Kethuboth* 111*b*, after Psalm lxxii. 16). Those that are buried elsewhere will therefore be compelled to creep through cavities in the earth until they reach the Holy Land (*Pesikta rabbah* i., with reference to Ezek. xxxvii. 13; *Kethuboth* 111*a*)."[1] Here again we meet with Particularistic views (in later times Universalistic ideas on the subject came to the fore, see below), and

[1] *Jewish Encycl.* x. 383*b*.

this is further illustrated by the fact that it was taught that in order that *all* Israel might partake of the joys of the Messianic Kingdom, those who had died before the coming of the Messiah and who were gathered in Sheol, would be brought up from there; the one condition was that they should have the mark of the Covenant (*i.e.* Circumcision); this, of course, precluded the Gentiles, according to the early Rabbinical view, from hoping for the Resurrection. It was further taught that all those who are imprisoned in Sheol should be brought out by the Messiah, who Himself would come and fetch them thence (*cf.* 1 Pet. iii. 19);[1] in *Bereshith rabbah* we read: "And when they that were bound in Gehinnom saw the light of the Messiah, they rejoiced in receiving Him, and said, This is He who will lead us out of darkness" (see Jellinek, *Beth Hamidrash* ii. 50). After they have been brought out of Sheol there will follow the Resurrection of the Just. God, it is said further, will give the Messiah the "Key" of the Resurrection of the dead (*Sanhedrin* 113*a*). Elsewhere (*Jer. Targum* to Exod. xx. 15, cf. *Berachoth* 15*b*) it is said that the trumpet shall be blown to arouse the

[1] Weber, *op. cit.* p. 368.

dead, and that this will be the signal for the Resurrection. (*Cf.* Isa. xxvii. 13; 1 Cor. xv. 52; 1 Thess. iv. 16). Another interesting belief was that men would rise from the dead in the same clothes in which they had been laid in the tomb. In *Sanhedrin* 90*b* this is paralleled by the example of a grain of wheat, which does not come forth from the earth naked, but covered in its garment (*cf.* 1 Cor. xv. 37); and if this is so with a grain of wheat, how much more with the human body! It is for this reason that minute directions are given by dying Rabbis regarding the clothes in which they are going to be buried.[1] But in later times the circumscribed idea of the Resurrection of Israel alone gave way to that of a general Resurrection; "as in the course of time the national hope with its national resurrection and final day of judgement no longer satisfied the intellect and human sentiment, the resurrection assumed a more universal and cosmic character. It was declared to be solely the act of God, Who alone possesses the Key that will unlock the tombs (*Berachoth* 15*b*). . . . Nor is the wrath of the last judgement believed any longer to be brought upon the heathen solely as such.

[1] Weber, *op. cit.* p. 370.

All evil-doers who have blasphemed God and His Law, or acted unrighteously, will meet with their punishment (*Tos. Sanh.* xiii.; *Midr. Teh.* vi. 1, ix. 15)."[1]

§vi. *The Messianic Banquet.*

This has been referred to in chap. iii. v. and vi. §iv., where we saw that the subject is mentioned several times in the Apocalyptic literature; it plays a more prominent part in Rabbinical literature, thus, in the *Targum of Pseudo-Jonathan* to Num. xi. 26ff., in the prophecy of Eldad and Medad, we are told of this Messianic Banquet at which the Israelites will feast with great joy upon the ox that has been prepared for them for this purpose from the beginning. Bousset (*Die Religion des Judenthums im neutestamentlichen Zeitalter*, p. 271) mentions a parallel idea in Iranian Eschatology, according to which the marrow of the slain ox Hadhayos is to be the food of immortality for the Righteous. But it is in connection with Leviathan that the Messianic Banquet is usually referred to in Rabbinical literature; for example, in *Baba Bathra* 74*a*,

[1] *Jewish Encycl.* x. 384*a*.

it is said that at the time of the Resurrection a banquet will be given by God to the Righteous, and that at this feast the flesh of Leviathan will be eaten. Very quaint ideas of a haggadic character (*i.e.* didactic narrative) figure in this literature; according to one, it appears that prior to the Banquet the Righteous will take part in the hunting of Leviathan and Behemoth; the angel Gabriel has the task of slaying Leviathan, but he will not be able to accomplish it without the help of God, Who will therefore come and divide the monster with His sword. According to another haggadah, when Gabriel fails, God will order Leviathan to engage in a battle with the "ox of the mountain," which will result in the death of both of them (*Baba Batha 75a*); then Leviathan will be cut up and eaten by the Righteous. These haggadahs are probably based upon such passages as Isa. xxvii. 1: *In that day the Lord with his sore and great and strong sword shall punish Leviathan the swift serpent, and Leviathan the crooked serpent; and he shall slay the dragon that is in the sea?* Psalm lxxiv. 12-15: . . . . *Thou didst break the heads of the Leviathan, thou wilt give him for food* . . . .;[1] Job. xxvi.

[1] Cf. *The Evolution of the Messianic Idea*, p. 53.

12, 13, and others. As Leviathan represents the principle of evil, his destruction symbolises the end of sin;[1] the banquet on his flesh, which is a much later idea, is interpreted by Maimonides as being an allusion to the spiritual enjoyment of the intellect;[2] originally it probably connoted something far more materialistic, and it may be safe to say that it was based upon the ordinary custom of royal banquets.

§vii. *The Appearance of Elijah, the Forerunner.*

The thought of the "Forerunner" is so prominent in the Gospels that a brief reference to it as regards Jewish post-biblical literature will not be out of place here. The fact of Elijah's appearance is mentioned first in Mal. iv. 5: *Behold, I will send you Elijah the prophet before the great and terrible day of the Lord come;* though this is, of course, referred to in Mal. iii. 1, but Elijah is not mentioned by name there; and in the Gospels the words in Isa. xl. 3, are adapted to the same purpose,

[1] Cf. *The Evolution of the Messianic Idea*, pp. 185ff.
[2] *Jewish Encycl.* viii. 38*a*.

though in their original context the reference is to the historical conditions of the time: *The voice of one that crieth, Prepare ye in the wilderness the way of the Lord, make straight in the desert a highway for our God.* How firm the belief was, long before the Christian Era, that Elijah was to fill this office may be seen from Sir. xlviii. 4-10: "How wast thou glorified, O Elijah, in thy wondrous deeds! And who shall glory like unto thee? . . . Who was recorded for reproofs in their seasons, to pacify anger before it brake forth into wrath; to turn the heart of the father unto the son, and to restore the tribes of Jacob." According to a tradition contained in *Yalkut Shimeoni*, it is said in reference to Isa. lii. 7, that three days before the Advent of the Messiah, Elijah will appear upon the mountains of Israel, and will announce to the world that the time of peace is about to come; so loud will his voice be that it will be heard from one end of the earth to the other. According to *Erubin* 43*a*, Elijah will first present himself before the Sanhedrin when he comes. In connection with this it is interesting to note that at the appearance of John the Baptist, priests and Levites from Jerusalem, and therefore without doubt emissaries from the central

Jewish authorities, came to the Baptist in the wilderness to enquire who he was (John i. 19: *And this is the witness of John, when the Jews sent unto him from Jerusalem priests and Levites to ask him, Who art thou?*). But the most important part of the Rabbinical teaching on the subject is that Elijah will lead the Jews to repentance when he appears; thus in *Pirqe de-Rabbi Elieser* c. 43, it says: "Israel will not bring forth the 'great repentance' before Elijah comes"[1] (see Luke i. 16, 17).

[1] For these references to the Rabbinical literature see Weber, *op. cit.* pp. 352ff., *Jewish Encycl.* v. 126ff., where many more examples will be found.

CHAPTER VIII.

THE COMING OF THE MESSIAH, THE SON OF MAN.

WE have dealt hitherto almost exclusively with pre-Christian teaching; but we proceed now a step further, and in examining the subject of the Advent of the "Son of Man," we shall, while starting from the Old Testament and Apocalyptic literature, be here mainly occupied with the Gospel teaching. The consideration of the history of the title "the Son of Man" affords a natural transition from Jewish to Christian Eschatology; and while it is far from our intention to study exhaustively the history of this title, some little detail will, nevertheless, be necessary.

We must first of all deal with the seventh chapter of the book of Daniel;[1] in verses 13, 14 of this chapter we read as follows:

[1] The phrase "son of man" which occurs frequently in the book of Ezekiel, is merely a mode of address, and has nothing to do with the present subject.

I saw in the night visions, and, behold, there came with the clouds of heaven one like unto a son of man, and he came even unto the Ancient of Days, and they brought him near before him. And there was given him dominion, and glory, and a kingdom, that all the peoples, nations, and languages should serve him: his dominion is an everlasting dominion, which shall not pass away, and his kingdom that which shall not be destroyed.

Here it is to be noted that this one who is "like unto a son of man" comes "*with* the clouds of heaven"; it is no fanciful distinction when one points out the difference between coming *upon* the clouds, and coming *with* the clouds; the former is only used of God Almighty (*e.g.*, Isa. xxi. 1; Psalm civ. 3). There is, therefore, some reason in the writer's mind for using the expression *with* the clouds, instead of *upon* the clouds. And the reason is not far to seek; the meaning of the vision is that the future world-ruler is to be not from the earth, but from Heaven; that is to say, the coming rule or kingdom is to be divinely appointed, and it is to be a *human* rule, hence the expression "a son of man"; and here again it is very important to notice that the phrase "a son of man" is widely different from "The Son of Man"; the former, "a son of man," is merely the Aramaic way of expressing a "human being"; and the point of the vision is that it declares that the ruler in this coming kingdom, though sent by God (and in that sense from Heaven), is a human being. In the vision the contrast is brought out between the beasts arising out of the sea, who are symbolic of the world-powers that have been, and the one who is like unto a son of man, *i.e.*, who is symbolic of the future ruler of the kingdom to come. But it is an earthly kingdom; and from the twenty-seventh verse of this chapter it is plain that this one who is like unto a son of man symbolises the Israelite nation: *And the kingdom, and the dominion, and the greatness of the kingdoms under the whole heaven, shall be given to the people of the saints of the Most High; his kingdom is an everlasting kingdom, and all dominions shall serve and obey him* (see, too, verses 18-22). Thus, while the title "Son of Man" is originally derived from this passage in the book of Daniel, it does not there denote anything more than that he to whom it is applied is a *human being*.

The next step in the history of the title "Son of Man" is its consideration in that portion of *Ethiopic Book of Enoch* called the *Similitudes, i.e.*, chaps. xxxvii.-lxx.; these belong approximately, as we have already seen, to 94-64 B.C.

In the first place, the "Son of Man" is here spoken of as existing before the beginning of the world: "At that hour that Son of Man was named before the Lord of Spirits, and his name before the Ancient of Days. Before the sun and the signs (of the Zodiac) were created, before the stars of Heaven were made his name was uttered before the Lord of Spirits.[1] He shall be a staff for the righteous and for the holy ones, that they may rest on him and not fall; he shall be the light of the Gentiles,[2] and the hope of those who are sad at heart.[3] . . . For this reason hath he been chosen and hidden before Him (*i.e.*, God) before the world was created, and unto eternity (he shall be) before Him. And the wisdom of the Lord of Spirits hath revealed him to the holy and righteous . . ." (xlviii. 2-7). To this belief in the pre-existence of the "Son of Man" before the creation of the world must be added the conception of his Kingdom,

[1] *Cf.* further Kautzsch, *Die Apokryphen und Pseudepigraphen des AT.* I. 264, note.

[2] See Isa. xlii. 6; xlix. 6; John viii. 12.

[3] *Cf.* Matt. xi. 28.

which is to be a universal one; he is described as, in a very real sense, the king of kings; for example, in the *Similitudes* lxii. 3ff., we read: "And there will stand up in that day all the kings and the mighty, and the exalted, and those who hold the earth, and they will see and recognise him as he sits on the throne of his glory. . . . And the kings and the mighty and all who possess the earth will glorify and bless and extol him who rules over all—who was hidden . . ." (verses 2-9, *cf.* xlv. 4-5). The idea of this universal dominion is further emphasised by the fact that the Son of Man is described as sitting upon the throne of God Almighty: "And the Chosen One shall sit upon My throne in those days, and all the secrets of wisdom will come forth from the thoughts of his mouth; for the Lord of Spirits hath given it to him, and hath glorified him."[1] One other point, which is of especial importance for our present purpose, is that this Son of Man is described as coming to judge the world: "He (the Son of Man) sat himself upon the throne of his glory, and the sum of judgement was committed unto him, the Son of Man, and he caused the sinners and they that have led the world

[1] See John xvii. 1, 5.

astray to disappear from the face of the earth and to be destroyed; with chains shall they be bound, and they shall be imprisoned in the place where they shall be gathered together (a place of) destruction" (lxix. 27, 28; lxii. 3-5). That this throne is God's throne is clear from li. 3; "And the Chosen One will in those days sit upon My throne. . . ." How exactly these thoughts are reflected in the Gospels will already have been realised, but it may be well to illustrate this very briefly. The pre-existence of the Son of Man is taught in the Gospels, for example, in John xvii. 24: *Father, that which thou hast given me, I will that, where I am, they also may be with me; that they may behold my glory, which thou hast given me; for thou lovedst me before the foundation of the world* (*cf.* John xvii. 5). The universality of His kingdom as taught in the Gospels is seen, for example, in Matt. xxviii. 18, 19: *And Jesus came unto them and spake unto them, saying, All authority hath been given unto me in heaven and on earth. Go ye therefore, and make disciples of all nations. . . .* Further, for the thought of the Son of Man sitting upon the throne of God, one recalls such words as those contained in Matt. xxv. 31: *But when the Son of Man shall come in his glory, and all the angels with him, then shall he sit on the throne of his glory* (*cf.* Matt. xix. 28); especially when one reads this in connection with such a passage as John xvii. 5: *And now, O Father, glorify me with thy own self with the glory which I had with thee before the world was.* And, lastly, for the truth that the Son of Man will come to judge, see John v. 22: *For neither doth the Father judge any man, but he hath given all judgement unto the Son;* John v. 27: *And he gave him authority to execute judgement, because he is the Son of Man;* John v. 30: *My judgement is righteous.*

It will be seen, on comparing the conception of the "Son of Man" in the book of Daniel with that contained in this section of *Eth. Enoch* (*i.e.*, the *Similitudes*), that there is a vital difference between the two; for in the former the "Son of Man" appears as the type or symbol of the nation of Israel; his *human* personality is emphasised; while in the latter he is presented as a *supernatural* person. Moreover, in the former the indefiniteness of the phrase "like unto a son of man," is very different from the distinct "the Son of Man" in the latter. Very important is the fact, therefore, that in the *Similitudes* of Enoch we meet for the *first time* with the title "The Son of Man." That is to say that, roughly speaking, eighty years before the birth of Christ, we have a presentation of a personality, called the "Son of Man," who is believed to have existed before the creation of world, whose kingdom is to be a universal one, who sits upon the throne of God, and who is described as coming to be the Judge of the world.

That in both the book of Daniel and in the *Similitudes* of Enoch the title, "The Son of Man," is used in reference to the Messiah does not require formal proof; it is only necessary to read the passages in question in order to see that the fact is obvious; the Messiah and "The Son of Man" are identical.[1]

Now we have next to consider the title of "The Son of Man" in the Gospels. The first point to notice, and it is a highly significant one, is that this title is never used excepting by our Lord Himself; an exception, the solitary one that exists, is seen in John xii. 34, where the multitude use it; but even here it is clear that they are only quoting words which Christ had used concerning Himself: *The multitude therefore answered him,*

[1] For a very valuable contribution to the history of the title Son of Man in pre-Christian literature, see Dalman, *Die Worte Jesu*, pp. 191-210.

We have heard out of the law that Christ abideth for ever: and how sayest thou, The Son of Man must be lifted up? Who is this Son of Man? The only time in which it is used in the New Testament outside the Gospels is in Acts vii. 56, where St. Stephen says: *Behold, I see the heavens opened, and the Son of Man standing on the right hand of God;* but these words, spoken before the Sanhedrin, are in reality a quotation of words of similar import which our Lord Himself had used before the same assembly:[1] *But from henceforth shall the Son of Man be seated at the right hand of the power of God* (Luke xxii. 69); so that in this case, too, the title is only used in a quotation of our Lord's own words concerning Himself.[2]

Next, we must see in what connection our Lord uses the title; and here we shall have to notice that there are two entirely different sets of ideas which He uses in connection with it. This is very striking, and at first, not altogether easy to understand. Firstly, our Lord uses the title "Son of Man" in regard

[1] *Cf.* Dalman, *Die Worte Jesu,* p. 206.

[2] The phrase which occurs in Rev. i. 13, xiv. 14, is used in the same sense as in the book of Ezekiel; while in Heb. ii. 6 it refers only to one who is of the human race; *i.e.,* in the one case it is a mode of address, in the other a way of describing one born of a woman.

to Himself in such a manner as to make it appear as though it were a term of humiliation; this will be clear in recalling such words as these: *The foxes have holes, and the birds of the heaven have nests; but the Son of Man hath not where to lay his head* (Matt. viii. 20; Luke ix. 58); *The Son of Man came eating and drinking, and they say, Behold, a gluttonous man, and a wine-bibber, a friend of publicans and sinners* (Matt. xi. 19; Luke vii. 34); speaking against the Son of Man is forgiven, not so if the Holy Spirit is spoken against (Matt. xii. 32; Luke xii. 10); the *suffering* of the Son of Man is referred to by Christ in a number of passages (Matt. xvii. 12; Mark viii. 13; Luke ix. 22; John iii. 14, etc.); so, too, His betrayal; and Christ says that, *The Son of Man came not to be ministered unto, but to minister, and to give his life a ransom for many* (Matt. xx. 28; Mark x. 45). All these passages speak of the "Son of Man" in connection with suffering and humiliation; and if the Gospels contained only passages like those just referred to, when speaking of the "Son of Man," we should be wholly justified in regarding the title "Son of Man" as indicating our Lord's human nature in contrast to passages which speak of Him as the "Son of God," as laying stress on His Divine Nature. But there are a considerably larger number of passages in which the title is used in connection with the ideas of glory, honour, and majesty. To give but a few examples: The Son of Man is able to forgive sins (Matt. ix. 6, etc.); He is Lord of the Sabbath (Mark ii. 28, etc.); it is He Who sows the good seed, in the parable of the wheat and tares (Matt. xiii. 24-30); but above all, and this is exceedingly important, almost always when Christ speaks of His *Second Coming* He uses the title of the Son of Man, this more than thirty times in the Gospels; and among these passages it is very interesting to notice how frequently the thought of His coming *to judge the world* is either prominent or understood without being actually expressed. Only one or two examples of this need be cited: *For the Son of Man shall come in the glory of his Father with his angels; and then shall he render unto every man according to his deeds* (Matt. xvi. 27, 28); *And then shall he send forth the angels, and shall gather together his elect from the four winds, from the uttermost part of the earth to the uttermost part of heaven* (Mark xiii. 27); *For whosoever shall be ashamed of me and of my words, of him shall the Son of Man be ashamed, when he cometh in his own glory, and the glory of the Father, and of the holy angels* (Luke xi. 26); and just one other striking passage: *But when the Son of Man shall come in his glory, and all the angels with him, then shall he sit on the throne of his glory; and before him shall be gathered all the nations; and he shall separate them one from another, as the shepherd separateth the sheep from the goats* (Matt. xxv. 31, 32). The judgement-scene that follows will be familiar, and need not be further dealt with here.

The following table, which contains all the passages of the Gospels in which the title "The Son of Man" is used, will fully illustrate what has just been said.

Passages in which the title "The Son of Man" is used in connection with the ideas of *suffering and humiliation*:—

Matt. viii. 20: And Jesus said unto them, The foxes have holes, and the birds of heaven have nests, but the Son of Man hath not where to lay his head. (*Cf.* Luke ix. 58.)

Matt. xi. 19: The Son of Man came eating and drinking, and they say, Behold a gluttonous man, and a wine-bibber, a friend of publicans and sinners (*Cf.* Luke vii. 34.)

Matt. xii. 32: And whosoever shall speak a word against the Son of Man, it shall be forgiven him; but whosoever shall speak against the Holy Spirit, it shall not be forgiven him, neither in this world nor in that which is to come. (*Cf.* Mark iii. 28-31; Luke xii. 10.)

Matt. xii. 40: For as Jonah was three days and three nights in the belly of the whale; so shall the Son of Man be three days and three nights in the heart of the earth. (*Cf.* Luke xi. 30-32.)

Matt. xvi. 13: . . . He asked his disciples, saying, Who do men say that the Son of Man is? (*Cf.* Mark viii. 27; Luke ix. 18; the context in each case points to the idea of the Suffering Christ.)

Matt. xvii. 12, 13: . . . But I say unto you that Elijah is come already, and they knew him not, but did unto him whatsoever they listed. Even so shall the Son of Man also suffer of them. (Mark ix. 12, 13.)

Matt. xvii. 22, 23: The Son of Man shall be delivered up into the hands of men; and they shall kill him, and the third day he shall be raised up. And they were exceeding sorry. (Matt. xx. 18, 19; Mark viii. 31; ix. 31, 32; x. 33, 34; Luke ix. 22, 44; xviii. 31-34.)

Matt. xx. 28: The Son of Man came not to be ministered unto, but to minister, and to give his life a ransom for many. (Mark x. 45.)

Matt. xxvi. 2: Ye know that after two days the passover cometh, and the Son of Man is delivered up to be crucified.

Matt. xxvi. 24: The Son of Man goeth, even as it is written of him; but woe unto that man by whom the Son of Man is betrayed. (Mark xiv. 21; Luke xxii. 22.)

Matt. xxvi. 45: Then cometh he to the disciples and saith unto them, Sleep on now, and take your rest; behold, the hour is at hand, and the Son of Man is betrayed into the hands of sinners. (Mark xiv. 41.)

Luke vi. 22: Blessed are ye, when men shall hate you, and when they shall separate you from their company, and reproach you, and cast out your name as evil, for the Son of Man's sake. (*Cf.* Matt. v. 11.)

Luke xxii. 48: But Jesus said unto him, Judas, betrayest thou the Son of Man with a kiss?

Luke xxiv. 6-7: Remember how he spake unto you when he was yet in Galilee, saying that the Son of Man must be delivered up into the hands of sinful men, and be crucified, and the third day rise again.

John iii. 13, 14, 15: And no man hath ascended into heaven, but he that descended out of heaven, even the Son of Man [which is in Heaven].[1] And as Moses lifted up the serpent in the wilderness, even so must the Son of Man be lifted up; that whosoever believeth in him may have eternal life.

John viii. 28: Jesus therefore said, When ye have lifted up the Son of Man, then shall ye know that I am he, and that I do nothing of myself, but as the Father taught me, I speak these things.

[1] The words in square brackets are not well attested.

John xii. 34: The multitude therefore answered him, We have heard out of the law that the Christ abideth for ever; and how sayest thou, The Son of Man must be lifted up? Who is this Son of Man?

Passages in which the title "The Son of Man" is used in connection with the ideas of *power, glory, and honour*:—

Matt. ix. 6: But that ye may know that the Son of Man hath power on earth to forgive sins (then saith he to the sick of the palsy), Arise, and take up thy bed, and go into thy house. (Mark ii. 10, 11; Luke v. 24.)

Matt. x. 23: Verily, I say unto you, Ye shall not have gone through the cities of Israel, till the Son of Man be come.

Matt. xii. 8: The Son of Man is lord of the Sabbath. (Mark ii. 28; Luke vi. 8.)

Matt. xiii. 37: He answered and said, He that soweth the good seed is the Son of Man.

Matt. xiii. 41, 42: The Son of Man shall send forth his angels, and they shall gather out of his kingdom all things that cause stumbling, and them that do iniquity, and shall cast them into the furnace of fire.

Matt. xvi. 27, 28: For the Son of Man shall come in the glory of his Father with his angels; and then shall he render unto every man according to his deeds. Verily, I say unto you, There be some of them that stand here, which shall in no wise taste of death, till they see the Son of Man coming in his kingdom.

Matt. xvii. 9: Jesus commanded them, saying, Tell the vision to no man, until the Son of Man be risen from the dead. (Mark ix. 9; *cf.* Luke ix. 35, 36.)

Matt. xix. 28: And Jesus said unto them, Verily, I say unto you, That ye which have followed me, in the regeneration, when the Son of Man shall sit on the throne of his glory, ye also shall sit upon twelve thrones, judging the twelve tribes of Israel.

Matt. xxiv. 27: For as the lightning cometh forth from the east, and is seen even unto the west, so shall be the coming of the Son of Man. (Luke xvii. 22-24.)

Matt. xxiv. 29-31: But immediately after the tribulation of those days, the sun shall be darkened, and the moon shall not give her light, and the stars shall fall from heaven, and the powers of the heavens shall be shaken; and then shall appear the sign of the Son of Man in heaven; and then shall all the tribes of the earth mourn, and they shall see the Son of Man coming on the clouds of heaven with power and great glory. And he shall send forth his angels with a great sound of a trumpet, and they shall gather together his elect from the four winds, from one end of heaven to the other. (Mark xiii. 24-27.)

Matt. xxiv. 37-44: And as were the days of Noah, so shall be the coming of the Son of Man. For as in those days which were before the flood they were eating and drinking, marrying and giving in marriage, until the day that Noah entered into the ark, and they knew not until the flood came, and took them all away; so shall it be in the coming of the Son of Man. . . . . . . Therefore be ye also ready; for in an hour that ye think not the Son of Man cometh. (Luke xii. 40; xvii. 26-37.)

Matt. xxv. 31-33: But when the Son of Man shall come in his glory, and all the angels with him, then shall he sit on the throne of his glory, and before him shall be gathered all the nations; and he shall separate them one from another, as a shepherd separateth the sheep from the goats; and he shall set the sheep on his right hand, and the goats on the left. (*Cf.* Luke xxi. 27, 28, 36.)

Matt. xxvi. 64: Nevertheless I say unto you, Henceforth ye shall see the Son of Man sitting at the right hand of power, and coming on the clouds of Heaven. (Mark xiv. 62; *cf.* xxii. 69.)

Mark viii. 38: For whosoever shall be ashamed of me and of my words in this adulterous and sinful generation, the Son of Man also shall be ashamed of him when he cometh in the glory of his Father with the holy angels. (Luke ix. 26; *cf.* xii. 8.)

Luke xviii. 8: Howbeit when the Son of Man cometh, shall he find faith on the earth?

Luke xix. 10: For the Son of Man came to seek and to save that which was lost.

John i. 51: And he saith unto him, Verily, verily, I say unto you, Ye shall see the heaven opened, and the angels of God ascending and descending upon the Son of Man. (*Cf.* John vi. 62.)

John vi. 27: Work not for the meat which perisheth, but for the meat which abideth unto eternal life, which the Son of Man shall give unto you; for him the Father, even God, hath sealed. (*Cf.* John vi. 53.)

John xii. 23, 24: And Jesus answereth them, saying, The hour is come, that the Son of Man should be glorified. Verily, verily, I say unto you, except a grain of wheat fall into the earth and die, it abideth by itself alone; but if it die, it beareth much fruit. (*Cf.* John xiii. 31.)

These facts regarding Our Lord's use of the title "The Son of Man" in regard to Himself present us, therefore, with a problem which is well worth pondering. The intimate connection between humiliation and glory, between the Sufferer and the Judge, which the title "The Son of Man" connotes in the mouth of our Lord, must obviously be intentional, a great truth must underlie the whole thing—the question is, Can we fathom it? Nothing can be clearer than that it utterly puzzled the disciples; but it is also certain that we are to-day in a better position to unravel the problem than can have been the case with the disciples.

We shall find ourselves assisted more than half-way by recalling the words of our Lord, after His Resurrection, to the two disciples whom He met on the way to Emmaus; He said unto them: *O foolish men, and slow of heart to believe in all that the prophets have spoken! Behoved it not the Christ to suffer these things, and to enter into his glory? And beginning from Moses and from all the prophets he interpreted to them in all the scriptures the things concerning himself.* (Luke xxiv. 25-27.) What must strike one here, first of all, is that our Lord refers to the past; He says, almost in so many words, that there is really nothing new, nothing to be surprised at, in all that had happened, because it was the fulfilment and realisation of what the prophets had spoken of long ago. It is certain, therefore, that for a solution of the problem before us we must look to the past; and in the words just quoted—"Behoved it not the Christ to suffer these things, and to enter into his glory?"—the two great thoughts concerning the Messiah in the past are summed up. The first is to be found in the book of Isaiah, the second in the book of Enoch. Does it offend some to hear this? "What is this book of Enoch," some will say, "that is thus coupled with the book of Isaiah? How can a book that does not even belong to the *Apocrypha* (let alone the canonical Scriptures) be mentioned side by side with that which stands first among the Old Testament books?" Some people have put the question in another way: "How comes it that the book which contains the most wonderful account of the Son of Man from the point of view of His majesty and glory, which describes the Advent of the Son of Man in terms practically identical with those of the Gospels — how comes it that such a book was never admitted into the Old Testament Canon? No doubt the Pharisees and the Scribes could have told us. Be that as it may, of this fact there can be no doubt: that as the book of Isaiah foretells the Gospel story of the Suffering Messiah in a way that no other book does, so does the book of Enoch describe the Gospel account of the coming of the Son of Man in His glory in a way that no other book does. When, therefore, we find that in the Gospels the Son of Man appears, on the one hand, as humiliated, the object of scorn, and the Sufferer, and, on the other hand, as the glorious King and Judge, it means that the prophecies of both the book of Isaiah and the book of Enoch find their fulfilment in Christ, the Son of Man, and Christ, the Son of God. *Behoved it not the Christ to suffer these things and to enter into His glory?— His visage was so marred more than any man; and his form more than the sons of men* (Isa. liii. 14); there we get the connection with the expression "son of man," but it is purely human. Again, *He was despised and rejected of men; a man of sorrows and acquainted with grief* (Isa. liii. 3); *he was wounded for our transgressions, he was bruised for our iniquities; the chastisement of our peace was upon him; and with his stripes we are healed . . . the Lord hath laid on him the iniquity of us all* (verses 5, 6). And the other seer said: "The Son of Man sat himself upon the throne of his glory, and the sum of judgement was committed unto him" (*Eth. Enoch* lix. 27); "And there will stand up in that day all the kings and the mighty, the exalted, and they that possess the land; they shall see and know him when he sits upon the throne of his glory, and righteous judgement shall there be in his presence, and no lie shall be spoken before him" (*Eth. Enoch* lii. 3).[1]

As in days of old, so now: "We believe that Thou shalt come to be our Judge"; but as in days of old, so now: "We pray Thee, therefore, help Thy servants, whom Thou hast redeemed with Thy precious blood." Our redemption is through His suffering; but the Judge comes in glory.

[1] These are only a very few of the appropriate passages which could be cited.

The problem connected with the title of "The Son of Man" in the Gospels may thus be explained by saying that Christ teaches the doctrine of His Human and Divine nature by accepting the prophecies which had gone before concerning the Son of Man, and regarding them as applying to Himself; and His use of the title may therefore be said to sum up diverse and apparently contradictory ideas which had long been in existence, but which, as was inevitable, men had very inadequately understood.

We must next turn to the Gospel teaching concerning the four main elements of the Eschatological Drama, together with the other less important points, which we considered in the Old Testament and in the Apocalyptic literature.

CHAPTER IX.

THE GOSPEL TEACHING OF THE SECOND ADVENT.

THE Gospel teaching of the Second Advent, as far as the four main points already referred to are concerned, is so familiar that on reading the passages given above from the Old Testament and the Apocalyptic literature which deal with the antecedents of this teaching, passages from the Gospels will have spontaneously suggested themselves; therefore it will not be necessary to give many quotations. Nevertheless, for purposes of illustration a certain number of passages must be cited; this will also serve to show more clearly the identity of thought between the Gospel teaching and that which preceded, on certain fundamental points. We shall take the four main elements in the same order as in chaps. ii. and v.; comparisons can then be very easily made with the corresponding sections in each; the subsidiary points of interest referred to in previous chapters will also be dealt with here. It should, however, be mentioned in passing that points of similarity with antecedent teaching only constitute one aspect of the Gospel teaching; we shall, in the next chapter, draw attention to another aspect, according to which it presents important points of contrast with the earlier teaching.

§i. *The Signs which precede the End.*

The most striking of these are the physical phenomena which are to herald the approach of Christ, thus in Luke xxi. 25, 26, we read: *And there shall be signs in sun, moon, and stars; and upon the earth distress of nations, in perplexity for the roaring of the sea and the billows; men fainting for fear, and for expectation of the things which are coming on the world; for the powers of the heavens shall be shaken* (*cf.* Matt. xxiv. 29; Mark xiii. 24; and see the quotation from Joel ii. 28-32 in Acts ii. 17ff.). In connection with these physical phenomena it is interesting to recall the words in Rev. vi. 12-17: . . . *and the sun became black as sackcloth of hair; and the whole moon became as blood, and the stars of the heaven fell unto the earth . . . and the heaven was removed as a scroll when it is rolled up; and every mountain and island were moved out of their places . . . and they say to the mountains and to the rocks, Fall on us, and hide us from the face of him that sitteth upon the throne, and from the wrath of the Lamb. . . .* Earthquakes and famine are other signs (see Matt. xxiv. 7; Mark xiii. 8). Further, universal fighting, not only war between nations, but also enmity between relatives and friends, are to be signs of the end—Matt. xxiv. 6, 7: *And ye shall hear of wars, and rumours of wars: see that ye be not troubled; for these things must needs come to pass; but the end is not yet. For nation shall rise against nation, and kingdom against kingdom. . . .* The conflict between near relations is described, for example, in Matt. x. 21.: *And brother shall deliver up brother to death, and the father his child; and children shall rise up against their parents and cause them to be put to death*; so, too, in verses 35, 36, of the same chapter: *For I came to set a man at variance against his father; and the daughter against her mother, and the daughter-in-law against her mother-in-law, and a man's foes shall be they of his own household.* It will be noticed on comparing these words with the parallel ones in the earlier literatures that the similarity amounts often to verbal identity. Another of the signs of the "last times" is the appearance of false Messiahs, thus in Matt. xxiv. 23, 24, we read: *Then if any man shall say unto you, Lo, here is the Christ, or, Here; believe it not. For there shall arise false Christs, and false prophets, and shall show great signs and wonders, so as to lead astray, if possible, even the elect.* This feature does not appear to be at all prominent in the earlier literature, but that it existed is probable, as it occurs in the Rabbinical literature, which reflects and reserves so many traditional beliefs (see above, chap. vii. §i).

§ii. *The Second Advent of the Messiah.*

In Jewish theology it is taught that above the earth there are seven heavens;[1] the highest of these, the seventh, is called *Araboth*; this is the dwelling-place (or *Mechiza*) of God. But not only does the Almighty dwell here, the angels who serve Him are there, and also the souls of the righteous (*Chagigah* 15*b*; see Weber, *op. cit.* pp. 162ff.). But there are, so it is taught, three divisions in this "seventh

[1] *Cf.* 2 Cor. xii. 2.

heaven"; God Himself dwells in the innermost division, which is hidden from view by a *pargôd* ("curtain") of clouds; the righteous are in the next division,[1] and the angels in the outermost. Behind the *pargôd* of clouds, where God dwells, is the heavenly throne together with the "glory" of God. The "glory" of God is said to dwell upon the divine throne, and is often used for the Personality of God Himself, especially in the *Targums*.[2] A further point of great interest is the fact that in the divine *Mechiza*, or "dwelling-place," no being may ever enter, with the one exception of *Metatron*,[3] who is permitted to enter and act as mediator between the Israelites and God by writing down their merits in the Divine Presence. This teaching, which is found in Rabbinical writings belonging to times subsequent to the beginning of Christianity, reflects nevertheless thoughts and beliefs which existed long before the Christian Era; they are, therefore, worth bearing in mind in considering a few Gospel passages relative to the Second Advent of

[1] Probably, as Weber suggests, this division is equivalent to Paradise, referred to by St Paul in 2 Cor. xii. 4.

[2] See further on this, Oesterley and Box, *op. cit.* pp. 191-194.

[3] Concerning this human-divine being see Oesterley and Box, *op. cit.* pp. 170-178.

Christ. In Matt. xxv. 31 we read: *But when the Son of Man shall come in his glory and all the angels with him, then shall he sit on the throne of his glory* (*cf.* Mark xii. 25, 26); again, in Matt. xxiv. 30: *And then shall appear the sign of the Son of Man in heaven . . . and they shall see the Son of Man coming on the clouds of heaven with power and great glory.* Here one may be permitted to suggest that "the sign of the Son of Man in heaven" refers to the "glory" to which reference was made above. It has been suggested that by this "sign" is meant that Christ would appear with or on the Cross (Bousset on Rev. i. 7), and that "if St Matthew had this in mind, the 'sign of the Son of Man' would mean the crucified Saviour appearing in the air."[1] This idea seems incongruous in view of the words "on the clouds of heaven with power and great glory"; for the Cross would be too suggestive of humiliation. But besides this, it must be remembered that the "glory of God," or the *Shekhinah*, was always regarded as the *sign* of the Divine Presence.[2] The words in Rev. i. 7 (*Behold, he cometh with the clouds*;

[1] Allen, *St. Matthew*, p. 259.
[2] For references see Oesterley and Box, *op. cit.* pp. 191ff.

and every eye shall see him, and they which pierced him; and all the tribes of the earth shall mourn over him), which are cited in support of the view that the "sign" means the crucified Saviour, do not necessarily do so, for the mention of those "which pierced him" may well have been made in order to emphasise the overwhelming difference there is to be between the humiliation of Christ while on earth and His glory when He shall appear again; His persecutors are to be witnesses of this; and when it says, further, "all the tribes of the earth shall mourn over Him," this is parallel to the words in Matt. xxiv. 30: *Then shall all the tribes of the earth mourn*, their reason for mourning being that Christ has come to judge them,[1] in contradistinction to the gathering together of the elect, described in the next verse (*cf.* Luke xxi. 28, where Christ reassures His own followers). The thought of the righteous elect dwelling in the divine *Mechiza* is illustrated by Matt. xix. 28: *Verily, I say unto you, that ye which have followed me, in the regeneration when the Son of Man shall sit on the throne of his glory, ye also shall sit upon*

[1] Cf. *Eth. Enoch* lxii. 5. "Pain will seize them when they see that Son of Man sit on the throne of His glory" (see also xlv. 3; lxix. 27.)

twelve thrones, judging the twelve tribes of Israel. Assuming, as one may justly do, that this Jewish belief of the *Mechiza* and its three divisions, existed in pre-Christian times, the thought of Christ coming with the angels and the saints would naturally suggest itself.

A distinctive feature of the Gospel teaching concerning the Second Advent which requires a brief mention, is the suddenness of the Messiah's coming; in Matt. xxiv. 27, for example, our Lord teaches: *For as the lightning cometh forth from the east, and is seen even unto the west, so shall be the coming of the Son of Man.* Closely connected with this suddenness of the Advent is its unexpectedness; more than one parable of eschatological content teaches this, and the frequent emphasis laid on the need of watching is, of course, due to this feature. (See, for example, Matt. xxiv. 37-51, xxv. 13, and the parable of the Ten Virgins xxv. 1-12.)

§iii. *The Judgement on the Wicked.*

As in the parallel sections in the Old Testament and in the Apocalyptic literature, it is the *final* punishment of the Wicked that is here referred to. The most instructive and best known passage regarding this subject is Matt. xxv. 41 - 46; here, concerning the Wicked, it is said: *Then shall he say also unto them on the left hand, Depart from me ye cursed, into the eternal fire which is prepared for the devil and his angels. . . . And these shall go away into eternal punishment.* Again, Matt. xiii. 41, 42: *The Son of Man shall send forth his angels, and they shall gather out of his Kingdom all things that cause stumbling, and them that do iniquity, and shall cast them into the furnace of fire; there shall be the weeping and gnashing of teeth.* (*Cf.* verses 49, 50; Luke xiii. 28.) The strange idea of the "worm that dieth not," which we referred to in an earlier section (chap. ii. §iii.), occurs in reference to the Wicked in Mark ix. 48, where Gehenna is spoken of as the place *where their worm dieth not and the fire is not quenched.* The fire of Gehenna, or Hell, is referred to again in Mark ix. 43, and often in the Synoptic Gospels.

§iv. *The Blessedness of the Righteous.*

As in the preceding section, it will be only necessary to give one or two quotations to illustrate this subject. In Matt. xxv. 34 we read: *Then shall the King say unto them on his right hand, Come, ye blessed of my Father, inherit the Kingdom prepared for you from the foundation of the world;* so, too, in verse 46, ... *But the righteous* (shall go) *into eternal life.* Almost always, though there are one or two exceptions (Matt. viii. 11, Luke xiii. 28), the idea of the Israelites being in any way specially privileged is absent in the Gospel teaching; here Universalism has conquered Particularism, and this must have been one of the main reasons for the hatred felt by the Pharisees towards our Lord. The most striking passage, perhaps, in the Gospels illustrative of the Universalist spirit is Matt. xxiv. 31; *And he shall send forth his angels with a great sound of a trumpet, and they shall gather together his elect from the four winds, from one end of heaven to the other.* That the "elect" here are not to be understood as being restricted to those of Jewish race seems clear from the earlier part of this chapter, the whole of which is eschatological, for in verse 14 occur the words: *And this gospel of the Kingdom shall be preached in the whole world for a testimony unto all the nations; and then shall the end come.* The blessedness of the righteous, be they of whatsoever race, is also distinctly taught in the account of the great Judgement (xxv. 31-46) referred to above, for in verse 32 it says that before Him shall be gathered all nations; and He shall separate them one from another, as the shepherd separateth the sheep from the goats.

§v. *The Gathering of the Gentiles.*

As has been pointed out in an earlier chapter (vi. §i.), the Gospel teaching on this point is adumbrated in the *Ethiopic Book of Enoch* and in the *Testaments of the Twelve Patriarchs*; from the quotations already given from these two books it will have been seen that the attitude towards the Gentiles in the "last times" taken up is, with the rarest exceptions, Universalistic; they are to be gathered, not in order that they may be destroyed, but that they may be saved. Although here and there in the Gospels a Particularistic tendency may be discerned, it is altogether exceptional when this does occur; the general teaching is that without differentiating between Jew and Gentile, every soul that is fit for the Kingdom shall inherit it;

there are, indeed, some striking passages in which certain of the Jewish race are directly said to be *unfit* for the Kingdom; these only emphasise the Universalistic character of the Gospel teaching. As illustrative of how widely all men are embraced in the Gospel view of the Kingdom, no words could be more instructive than those in Matt. xxiv. 14: *And this gospel of the Kingdom shall be preached in the whole world for a testimony unto all the nations; and then shall the end come.* How entirely without any differentiation the Kingdom is promised to all who shall be found worthy is seen, for example, in Matt. xxv. 32ff. . . . . *And before him shall be gathered all the nations: and he shall separate them one from another, as the shepherd separateth the sheep from the goats* . . . (*cf.* Luke ii. 31, 32; xiii. 29); many other passages containing similar Universalistic teaching could be given. In one or two instances a special position of privilege seems to be accorded to the Jewish nation, thus in Matt. xix. 28 we read: *And Jesus said unto them, Verily I say unto you, that ye which have followed me, in the regeneration when the Son of Man shall sit on the throne of his glory, ye also shall sit upon twelve thrones, judging the twelve tribes of*

Israel; it must, however, be added, that the words which follow may legitimately be taken in a quite general sense, namely, *And every one that hath left houses or brethren . . . shall inherit eternal life.* Then, lastly, there are quite a number of instances in which it is said that the Jews will be cast out of the Kingdom on account of their unworthiness, and their places be taken by others; so, for example, Matt. viii. 12: *But the sons of the Kingdom shall be cast forth into the outer darkness: there shall be the weeping and gnashing of teeth.* Some of the parables quite clearly teach the same thing; thus in the parable of the householder who planted a vineyard we read at its close (Matt. xxi. 41): *He will miserably destroy those miserable men, and will let out the vineyard unto other husbandmen, which shall render him the fruits in their seasons*; the whole drift of the parable leaves no doubt as to who are intended by "those miserable men," and by the "other husbandmen," even if it were not made doubly clear by the words in verse 43: *Therefore I say unto you, The Kingdom of God shall be taken away from you, and shall be given to a nation bringing forth the fruits thereof.* (*Cf.* further Matt. xxi. 31; Luke xiii. 7-9.)

§vi. *The Ingathering of Israel.*

The ingathering of the dispersed Israelites all over the world is a regular feature in the Eschatology of the Old Testament and of the later literature; but from what has already been said we shall scarcely expect to see it figure prominently in the Gospels. One passage, it is true, which seems to be based on Isa. xxvii. 13, very probably did, in the first instance, refer to the dispersed Israelites, but it is a question whether the words were not deliberately chosen with a view to adapting them to a wider use; the passage is Matt. xxiv. 31: *And he shall send forth his angels with a great sound of a trumpet, and they shall gather together his elect from the four winds, from one end of heaven to the other.* It is more in accordance with the demand of true religion which, as the Gospel teaches, is the condition of entry into the Kingdom that we read in Luke iii. 7ff. . . . *Ye offspring of vipers, who warned you to flee from the wrath to come? Bring forth, therefore, fruits worthy of repentance, and begin not to say within yourselves, We have Abraham to our father; for I say unto you that God is able of these stones to raise up children unto Abraham.* . . . That the Jewish nation was intended to be the medium whereby salvation was to be brought to all men[1] seems definitely implied in such words as: *Salvation is of the Jews* (John iv. 22), and: *Go ye therefore, and make disciples of all nations, baptizing them* . . . (Matt. xxviii. 19); but this high privilege only emphasised the fact that their ingathering was to be conditioned by their spiritual state. See, further, the words in Matt. xix. 28: *Verily I say unto you, that they which have followed me, in the regeneration when the Son of Man shall sit on the throne of his glory, ye also shall sit upon twelve thrones, judging the twelve tribes of Israel.*

As an illustration of the spirit of the Gospel teaching, it is instructive to compare the thought of Israel being the medium of proclaiming, and bringing the knowledge of, salvation to all men, with the earlier idea which sometimes finds expression, of the Israelites being the instrument of punishing and destroying the Gentiles. (*Cf.* above, chap. ii. §iii.)

A feature that should be mentioned in connection with the ingathering of Israel is

[1] For this thought cf. *Sibylline Oracles* iii. 194ff., and see further above, chap. vi. §ii.

the state of the Temple in the time of bliss which is to be the lot of the Righteous; we have here an element concerning which the Gospel teaching and its antecedents are in striking contrast. In the Old Testament one great hope associated with the Messianic Age was that Jerusalem and the Temple would be rebuilt. Such prophecies as Ezek. xl.-xliv., xlvii., Isa. xxiv. 23, liv. 11ff., lx. 10ff., lxv. 17-19, which suggest the prospect of a new and glorious city and a restored Temple-worship, strongly fostered such hopes. In Hag. ii. 7-9 the consciousness that the second Temple (before its restoration by Herod) compared unfavourably with the first is already apparent. (*Cf.* also Tobit xiv. 5.) It was expected that a new and glorious Jerusalem would be built in the Messianic Age, of sapphires, gold, and precious stones, etc. (*Cf.* Tobit xiii. 15ff.; xiv. 4; Rev. xxi. 9-21.) This is identical with the "new" or "upper" Jerusalem ("the Jerusalem that is above," which is referred to in Gal. iv. 26, Hebr. xii. 22) which had been seen in vision by Adam, Abraham, and Moses (Syriac *Apocalypse of Baruch* iv. 26), and which was to be made manifest in all its glory by the Messiah (*cf. iv. Esdras* vii. 26, Syriac *Apocalypse of Baruch* xxxii. 4). In later times, after the complete destruction of both city and Temple, this hope came to even more vivid expression. (See, further, *Sibylline Oracles* iii. 286-290, 625-658 ; *Book of Jubilees* i. 29ff.; xxiii. 27ff.) The restoration of the Holy City, and especially of the Temple-worship, long continued to be an object of pious hopes and prayers; according to *Lev. rabbah* ix. the Messiah will Himself re-erect the Temple.[1] In view of such hopes and expectations, which with the building of Herod's Temple seemed to some extent realised, one can understand what must have been the feelings of those who, on drawing our Lord's attention to the buildings of the Temple, heard, in reply, the words: *See ye not all these things? Verily I say unto you, There shall not be left one stone upon another, that shall not be thrown down* (Matt. xxiv. 2).

The feature emphasises, again, the spiritual character of the Gospel teaching.

§vii. *The Resurrection of the Dead.*

In the earlier literature there is ambiguity as to the time of the Resurrection, as well as uncertainty as to who shall rise, whether it is

[1] Prayer for the restoration of the Temple-worship is offered in the Synagogue regularly at the present day (see Oesterley and Box, *op. cit.* p. 223).

to be the good alone, or the evil as well, and whether it is to be restricted to Israelites, or to men in general (see chaps. iii. §iv.; vi. §iii.; vii. §v.). According to the later teaching of the Jews the trumpet-blast which was to be the signal for the ingathering of the dispersed Israelites (*cf.* Isaiah xxvii. 13) would also rouse the sleeping dead (cf. *iv. Edras* iv. 23ff.; *Berachoth* 15*b*); in 1 Cor. xv. 52 we read: *For the trumpet shall sound, and the dead shall be raised incorruptible* . . . (see also 1 Thess. iv. 16). We are not concerned here with the doctrine of the Resurrection, but only with the *fact* of its mention in connection with eschatological thought. According to the Gospel teaching, it is only the Righteous who are to share in the Resurrection, for they who rise are "as the angels in heaven" (Luke xx. 35, 36), hence also the words, "the resurrection of the just" in Luke xiv. 14. It is, therefore, only the Righteous who rise, the Wicked are cast down into Gehenna (Matt. x. 28; Mark ix. 43ff.). It must be in the light of this that we are to understand the words in Matt. xxv. 46: *And these shall go away into eternal punishment, but the righteous into life eternal*, although direct mention of the Resurrection is not made here. Though it is not specifically stated (but see Matt. xxv. 32ff.), yet the whole spirit of the Gospel teaching shows that it knows no such distinction regarding the Resurrection of the Dead, as is implied in the words "Jew" and "Gentile." The passage (Matt. xxvi. 51-53) does not come into consideration here.

It may perhaps strike some as strange that the subject of the general Resurrection receives, comparatively speaking, such small notice in the Gospels. The reason, however, is not far to seek, for this belief was so firmly established among the Jews prior to the Christian Era as not to require specific treatment; it was one of those things which were naturally taken for granted, being an almost universally acknowledged fact; it was only on particular occasions, such as that referred to in Matt. xxii. 23ff., that the subject was dealt with in detail by Christ.

§viii. *The Messianic Banquet.*

There are some passages in the Gospels which suggest the idea of the Messianic Banquet, or something corresponding to it; but in each case the teaching is immeasurably more spiritual than what we read of in the earlier literature. One may well believe that the popular conception regarding this

Banquet was utilised by Christ and transformed, in order to teach a higher truth. It is possible that the thought of the Messianic Banquet lay behind the parable of the Marriage Feast (Matt. xxii. 1-14), see especially verse 13, where it is said that he who had not on a wedding-garment[1] was to be cast into the outer darkness, where there is *the weeping and gnashing of teeth.* (Cf. *Ascension of Isaiah* iv. 16.) More direct reference, however, may be discerned in Matt. viii. 11: *And I say unto you, that many shall come from the east and the west, and shall sit down with Abraham and Isaac, and Jacob . . .*; in the original "shall sit down" (literally "recline") is the regular word for reclining at a meal (*cf.* Luke xiii. 29). Significant, too, in this connection is the passage Luke xiv. 15-24, commencing with the words: *And when one of them that sat at meat with him heard these things, he said unto him, Blessed is he that shall eat bread in the kingdom of God. But he said, A certain man made a great supper . . .*; and the words in Matt. xxvi. 29 should also be

[1] With this thought of the "Wedding-garment" it is interesting to compare the mention of the "Garments of Life" in *Eth. Enoch* lxii. 16. (See also cviii. 12.)

considered: *But I say unto you, I will not drink henceforth of this fruit of the vine, until that day when I drink it new with you in my Father's Kingdom.*

In each of these passages the context shows that a new, a spiritual, meaning is being applied to the old traditional conception of the Messianic Banquet.

CHAPTER X.

THE GOSPEL TEACHING OF THE SECOND ADVENT:—CONTRAST WITH ITS ANTECEDENTS.

Having now briefly followed out the eschatological teaching of the Old Testament, the Apocalyptic literature, and the Gospels, and having illustrated each by quotations, we shall in the present chapter compare the Gospel presentation of the facts with the earlier teaching, and attempt to point out some of the main differences between the two; while in the next and concluding chapter we shall seek to account for what is, in spite of certain very pointed differences, the substantial identity in many particulars of the Eschatology of all three classes of literature.

§i. *The Central Figure in the Eschatological Drama.*

The first thing that naturally suggests itself

for consideration is the Personality of Him Who occupies the central position in the Eschatological Drama. In the Old Testament it is, as a rule, Jehovah Himself Who appears, sometimes as Judge of the Israelite nation (Amos v. 17), sometimes as Judge of all flesh (Isaiah lxvi. 15, 16), and at other times as the champion of His Chosen People (Isaiah lxv. 17-19). But this is not always so; in some of the most striking Messianic passages of the Old Testament the Central Personality alternates between Jehovah and His Anointed. The classical example of this is to be seen by comparing the following passages together, Isaiah ii. 2-4; iv. 2-6; ix. 5, 6; xi. 1-5; these four passages constitute what is in most respects the essence of the Old Testament Messianic teaching. In the first (ii. 2-4) Jehovah Himself is described as the Messianic Ruler; He is to be the universal Judge over all peoples. The Messianic Ruler is therefore divine, and His subjects are to include all nations. In the second passage (iv. 2-6) Jehovah is again represented as the Messianic Ruler on earth, but the method of His appearing is not of the same literal character as described in the earlier passage; it is indicated by the *Shekhinah*; His subjects are now restricted to those of the Children of Israel who have passed through a purifying process. In this passage, too, a new element enters into the circle of ideas, namely, the "Branch of Jehovah," forming the point of attachment for the idea of the "shoot," or "twig," of Jesse (Isaiah xi. 1, 10), and thus bringing in the connection of the house of David with the Messianic Ruler. In the third passage (ix. 5-6; 6-7 in the English Bible) it is a divine-human ruler—the Immanuel-conception in vii. 14 forming the link—who is to sit upon the throne of David; his subjects are to be the Children of Israel only. And in the fourth passage (xi. 1-5) a purely human ruler is presented, upon whom, however, the Spirit of Jehovah is manifest in a unique manner; he is a descendant of Jesse, and therefore presumably (though this is not explicitly stated) his subjects are restricted to the Children of Israel.[1] It seems, therefore, incontrovertible that, if one is to take these passages as they stand, in their natural meaning, and without reading into them thoughts and ideas which belong to later ages, one is forced to the conclusion that, at

[1] See for details concerning what is said here, *The Evolution of the Messianic Idea*, chaps. xiv., xv.

first, the prophet believed in the actual, visible presence of Jehovah Himself on earth when the "last times," which are to follow after the "signs," draw near; later on it is taught that Jehovah delegates this office to another. Other Old Testament writers also exhibit a similar uncertainty as to the Personality Who is to be the central figure in the "last times"; one of the latest passages in the Old Testament presents this idea of uncertainty, Mal. iii. 1: *Behold I send my messenger, and he shall prepare the way before me*—that is clear enough, referring as it does to the forerunner; but in the latter part of the verse we read: *And the Lord, whom ye shall seek, shall suddenly come to his temple; and the messenger of the covenant, whom ye delight in, behold he cometh, saith the Lord of Hosts;* the plain sense of the word requires one to differentiate between the "Lord" and the "messenger of the covenant"; and this differentiation seems natural when one remembers that uncertainty as to who the central figure in the Eschatological Drama is to be is characteristic of those Old Testament writers who deal with the subject. It is the same in the Apocalyptic writings, as will have been noticed in the passages which have been quoted in a previous chapter. Now when we come to the Gospel teaching we find no traces of any uncertainty in this matter; it is Christ, and Christ only, Who is the Central Figure in the "last times." Then, again, while in the earlier teaching it is always *Jehovah* who is to be the *Judge*—an office which is never committed to the Messiah of pre-Christian times,[1]—and the Messiah is always a human being,[2] in the Gospel teaching *Christ* is the *Judge*,[3] and He is also the Messiah; thus the Divine Judge and the human Messiah are found to be centred in the Person of Christ. This is the testimony which Christ bears of Himself: *But when the Son of Man shall come in his glory, and all the angels with him, then shall he sit on the throne of his glory, and before him shall be gathered all the nations; and he shall separate them one from another...* (Matt. xxv. 31-33); and on the other hand: *The Son of Man came not to be ministered unto, but to minister, and to give his life a ransom for many* (Mark x. 45). This point of

[1] We are, of course, only referring to the Judge in the restricted eschatological sense.

[2] It is true that the office of the Messiah, as ruler on earth, is sometimes, as we have seen, ascribed to Jehovah; but the Messiah Himself is always a human being in Old Testament teaching.

[3] Sometimes, in some of the parables, it is God Himself Who is the Judge (see Matt. xviii. 32; xx. 8; xxii. 11; Luke xviii. 7).

contrast between the antecedents of the Gospel teaching and this teaching itself is clearly of the highest importance; for it shows, on the one hand, that the earlier teaching was in some sense inadequate, but on the other hand, that it witnessed to a great truth. That the Christ's witness here concerning Himself implies that of His dual nature, the divine and the human, is sufficiently clear not to need further emphasis.

§ii. *The Time of the Second Advent.*

In the Old Testament and Apocalyptic writings the "last times" by no means always or necessarily imply the end of all things. Although *when* the "last times" are to come about is never definitely stated, they are always represented as a process upon which shall follow the inauguration of the new Age; but the scene of this new Age and the conditions under which it will be lived do not differ, excepting in one particular, very greatly from the conditions under which men have lived hitherto. The one particular is the *happiness* of that Age, and all that this involves; but it is not by any means always regarded as of unending duration; it will be lived on this earth, under very happy conditions, but under natural conditions. On the other hand, a development of belief took place; with a doctrine of the Resurrection, together with the conceptions expressed by the terms Gehenna, Paradise, Heaven, came the preparation for more spiritual ideas, and belief in a future life. This teaching, which thus connects the "last times" and the succeeding Messianic Kingdom with this earth, and here gradually develops a belief in the existence of the life to come, after the Resurrection and therefore in a sphere other than earthly—this teaching corresponds in some particulars with that of the Gospel; but the latter presents some marked points of contrast. According to the teaching of our Lord the Kingdom which He came to found came into being at His first Advent, and could therefore be spoken of as already present, *The Kingdom of Heaven is within you* (Luke xvii. 21; *cf.* Matt. vii. 13; xi. 12; xii. 25), and also as belonging to the future, *There be some of them that stand here, which shall in no wise taste of death, till they see the Kingdom of God* (Luke ix. 27; *cf.* Matt. vi. 6; viii. 11; Mark ix. 11; Luke xiii. 15); similarly we are to learn from this that the Kingdom is wholly spiritual, it is not a question as to whether it belongs to this world or to the world to come, because it stands outside of such considerations. The great differentiation which men make between this world and the next cannot come into consideration, in the same way, with God Who is spirit (*cf.* John iv. 24), for the kingdom has reference solely to the spiritual part of man's nature, and his spiritual attitude towards it as now present is the condition of his belonging to it hereafter: *Whosoever shall not receive the Kingdom of God as a little child, he shall in no wise enter therein* (Mark x. 15).

The chief point of contrast, therefore, so far, between the Gospel teaching and that which went before is that, according to the former, the Messianic Era, *i.e.*, the Kingdom of God, is established without the "signs" that precede the "last times," and without the various other elements which belong to the Eschatological Drama according to the presentment of the earlier literature (the only exception to this is that the forerunner appears in the Gospel as well as in the earlier teaching). These elements are presented in the Gospels in connection with Christ's *Second Advent*. But, according to the Gospel teaching, the Second Advent is really only to be the consummation of the Kingdom which the Messiah founded while on earth; this only serves to emphasise the truth that the "Kingdom to come" is only the continuation and more complete fulness and realisation of what has already been inaugurated on earth. The earlier teaching, as a rule, makes the establishment of the Kingdom and its consummation one and the same thing, or, at all events, very closely connected; but even here there is not always uniformity of teaching; for sometimes the sequence of events is: the "signs" which precede the end, the establishment of the Kingdom, the Resurrection and Judgement (sometimes these last two are interchanged); at other times the establishment and consummation of the Kingdom come last, and the Kingdom endures for ever. This uncertainty, in one respect, is reflected in the Gospel teaching, at least in so far as the time of the Second Advent is concerned; for it cannot be denied that the Second Advent (the technical term for this in the Gospels, and in the New Testament generally, is *Parousia*) is sometimes represented as about to take place within the present generation (see, *e.g.*, Matt. x. 23; xvi. 28; xxiv. 34; Mark viii. 28; ix. 1; Luke ix. 27), at other times it is implied that it will not be until some future, probably distant, date; this is certainly what must naturally be concluded from those passages which say that before the end comes the Gospel must be preached to all nations (*e.g.*, Mark xiii. 10; *cf.* Matt. xxviii. 19, 20). The difficulty is enhanced by the fact that the end of the world is sometimes identified with the destruction of Jerusalem. The full solution of these difficulties may perhaps be brought about by differentiating the various sources from which our Gospels in their present form have been compiled; but this is a precarious task, and one which cannot be touched upon here. It may legitimately be pointed out that according to our Lord's own testimony the time of His Second Advent was known only to the Father: *But of that day and hour knoweth no one, not even the angels of heaven, neither the Son* (the words "neither the Son" are omitted by some important authorities, but see Mark xiii. 32), *but the Father only* (Matt. xxiv. 36).

§iii. *The Character of the Kingdom.*

But if there is a certain similarity between the Gospel teaching and its antecedents in respect of the uncertainty of the actual time of the end, the two show a marked contrast between the conceptions which they respectively present concerning the character of the Kingdom. This is mainly seen in comparing the materialistic ideas of the earlier teaching with the spiritual teaching in the Gospels. In the Old Testament, as well as in the Apocalyptic literature, the Messianic Kingdom is described as a time in which material prosperity will be at its height, and the peace, which is another characteristic of this Kingdom, will be achieved by the overthrow and subjugation of the enemies of the Israelites; all nations are to bow down before them and acknowledge them as their masters; the Kingdom is a kingdom of this world. This is also the case in the more developed teaching of *Eth. Enoch*, see, *e.g.*, xxxviii. 4, 5: "And from that time those who possess the earth will no longer be powerful and exalted, and they will not be able to behold the face of the holy, for the light of the Lord of Spirits is seen on the face of the holy, and righteous and elect. Then will the kings and the mighty perish, and be given into the hand of the righteous and holy." But in the Gospel teaching everything that has to do with the Kingdom of God is of a spiritual character;

nothing could be in greater contrast to the earlier teaching than this. The Kingdom itself is described by Christ as *not of this world* (John xviii. 36), and therefore the happiness and peace of those who belong to it is of a spiritual kind. A *trait* which often occurs in the earlier literature is that in the time to come the righteous will look upon the wicked in their torments as though exulting over them; such an idea is, of course, wholly absent from the Gospel teaching, indeed it is a further point of contrast that the Gospels have far less to say about the judgement on the wicked than the earlier literature; the Gospel teaching is characterised by a much more pronounced note of hope;[1] nothing, for example, could be more striking than the words in the parable: *Go out quickly into the streets and lanes of the city, and bring in hither the poor and the maimed and blind and lame. . . . And the lord said unto the servant, Go out into the highways and hedges, and constrain them to come in . . .*; the Kingdom is as far as possible all-embracing; it is only, as it were, upon compulsion that the invincibly wicked

[1] It is true to say that the Apocalyptists were to a great extent driven by *despair* of better things on earth to frame their eschatological ideas; on the other hand, the basis of Gospel Eschatology is *hope*.

have to be cast out of it; even the wicked are included among the subjects of the Kingdom in the hope that they may thereby be leavened, and it is only at the very end, when they have consistently repudiated the gift of eternal life, that hope for them ceases; see the parables of the draw-net (Matt. xiii. 47-49), and of the leaven (Matt. xiii. 33).

The point of contrast here centres, therefore, in the fact of the wish that the wicked, by becoming better, should continue for ever as members of the Kingdom. They are not regarded as naturally shut out; on the contrary, it is taken for granted that in the normal course they *ought* to be included among its members.[1] According to the Gospel teaching every single human being is of account; and this brings us to another point of contrast between the earlier teaching and that of the Gospel regarding the Kingdom; it is that the importance of the individual is recognised in the latter, and practically ignored in the former; instead of the blessedness of *the Righteous* in the Kingdom, it is the blessedness of *the righteous one* that is emphasised in the Gospel teaching, each individual receiving

[1] Cf. 1 Tim. ii. 4: *Who willeth that all men should be saved, and come to the knowledge of the truth.*

recognition; and instead of the judgement on *the Wicked*, it is the judgement on *each wicked man* that is emphasised, each individual receiving judgement; this is a point of contrast which is of very great importance, and the significance of it cannot be overrated.

In summing up, therefore, the chief points of contrast between the Gospel teaching and that of its antecedents, we see, firstly, that there is no ambiguity as to the Personality of the Central Figure in the Eschatological Drama as presented in the Gospels; secondly, that the Gospel teaching is in every respect more spiritual than that of the earlier literature; thirdly, that the Gospel sounds a note of hope hitherto unknown; and fourthly, that in the Gospels the individual is raised to a place of importance which was not accorded him in earlier days. Besides this, it may also be added that much of the vagueness in the earlier literature is replaced by the more positive teaching of the Gospels, and the broad moral issues of the latter stand in marked contrast to a great deal of less important matter that figures in the antecedent teaching.

CHAPTER XI.

THE CHRISTIAN ADAPTATION OF JEWISH TEACHING.

Although, as we have seen in the preceding chapter, there are some important points of contrast between the Gospel teaching and that of its antecedents, nevertheless, as has already been pointed out, the former is in many respects identical with the latter, so that it is true to say that in many fundamental points the Gospel teaching concerning the Second Advent is to be found in pre-Christian Jewish writings. These points, which have been dealt with in earlier chapters, were: the *signs* of the Second Coming, the actual Advent, the Judgement upon the Wicked, the Reward of the Righteous, some other points of subsidiary importance, and the characteristics and Personality of the Son of Man, namely His pre-existence before the creation of the world, His universal Kingdom, His Kingship, and His character of Judge.

All this teaching, which we have been accustomed to regard as specifically Christian, we find already fully developed, not only in pre-Christian times, but for the most part in literature which is not regarded as being on the same level with the Old Testament Scriptures.

The question naturally arises, and presses for an answer: Is the Gospel teaching merely an adaptation of what was taught in certain unorthodox Jewish circles — for the *Book of Enoch*, for example, was never accepted as Scripture by the orthodox Pharisaic party? Or, if this is not so, what is one to say in view of the incontrovertible fact that a pre-Christian book, such as the one just mentioned, has, in many vital particulars, the identical teaching on the subject of the Second Advent as that of the Gospels? It is obvious that a great deal turns upon the answer to this question. There are not wanting those who maintain that the whole of the Gospel teaching concerning the Second Advent is to be taken in an allegorical, not in a literal sense; they would say that the struggles of conscience are the signs of the Advent, and that the spiritual entrance of Christ into our hearts is the real Second Coming; that when we are punished for our sins it is Christ's judgement upon us, and that peace of mind and the consciousness of doing what is right is Christ's reward of the just. That is to say, they regard the whole account as mystic allegory. They point out, further, that just as the Jews were mistaken in their conceptions concerning the promised Messiah, and just as the early Christians, including the Apostles themselves, were mistaken in their expectation of the almost immediate reappearance of Christ, so, too, Christians of to-day are mistaken in believing that Christ will actually come again in glory, with ten thousands of His angels. And they turn to us and say: "After all, your Gospel teaching on this subject is only the repetition of some erroneous Jewish notions, applied to Jesus Christ—erroneous Jewish notions found to a large extent in a book, to enhance the importance of which the author pretended was written by Enoch, the man of whom it was said that, 'he walked with God; and he was not; for God took him.'" How are we to answer statements of this kind? Merely to accuse those who make them of irreligion, blasphemy, or the like, is unscientific, unwise, and unchristian; the days in which a simple iteration of the faith was deemed sufficient are gone; we must give the reason of the hope that is in us; we must at least try and satisfy *ourselves*, even if we cannot satisfy others. And how is the average Christian going to answer to *himself* the objections which have just been pointed out, objections which the sceptical attitude of our age with regard to all belief urges with ever greater insistency? Certainly it is no easy matter; we are under the additional disadvantage of having to acknowledge that we can neither *prove* that our belief is right, nor that the objections of others are wrong; short of the actual coming to pass of the Second Advent, it is impossible to *prove* that the prophecies regarding it, contained in the Gospels or elsewhere, are true. Nevertheless, there are two prime considerations which, though far from constituting anything in the nature of a proof, do show the precariousness of the position taken up by those who reject as untenable the Gospel teaching concerning the Second Coming of Christ.

§i. It will be remembered that in a previous chapter great stress was laid upon two concurrent ideas which our Lord connects with the title of "The Son of Man"; His own words, which were quoted, showed that His use of that title connected it at one time with humiliation and suffering, at another with glory and majesty; and that when used with the latter it was almost always in connection with the Second Coming. It was, further, pointed out that in the words, "Behoved it not the Christ to suffer these things, and to enter into His glory," our Lord summed up two great prophecies concerning the Messiah in the past, viz., the conception of the "Suffering Servant," in *The Book of Isaiah*, and the conception of "The Son of Man" in His glory, in *The Book of the Similitudes of Enoch.*[1] Let us think of this for a little.

The picture of the "Servant of the Lord," with its most sublime description in Isa. liii., depicts, as we know, the ministering aspect of our Blessed Lord's life here on earth in a way which has bound thinking Christians with a holy fascination ever since the Resurrection of our Saviour; the reason of this has been not only the exquisite beauty and heart-moving pathos of the thoughts expressed, but the positively astounding accuracy of the prophecy as fulfilled in our Lord. A convinced sceptic, though one who possessed the historic sense, on having read the fifty-third

[1] *See* chap. viii.

chapter of Isaiah and then the life of our Lord, and being asked what he thought about it all, replied: "It looks as though the life were lived in order to fulfil the prophecy!" The answer was characteristic, but profoundly significant. Let only these few points of correspondence be recalled:—*He was despised and rejected of men; a man of sorrows, and acquainted with grief* (Isa. liii. 3); *And they smote his head with a reed, and did spit upon him . . . and they led him out to crucify him* (Matt. xv. 17, 20);—"despised and rejected!" And in His own words the Man of Sorrows cries: *My soul is exceeding sorrowful even unto death* (Mark xiv. 34). Again, *He was wounded for our transgressions, he was bruised for our iniquities . . . with his stripes we are healed; all we like sheep have gone astray . . . and the Lord hath laid on him the iniquity of us all* (Isa. liii. 5, 6); the fact that words like these were so alien to the Jewish conception of atonement makes it all the more wonderful when we read them in the light of such sayings as these: *This cup is the new covenant in my blood, even that which is poured out for you* (Luke xxii. 20); *I am the good shepherd: the good shepherd layeth down his life for the sheep* (John x. 11). Once more; the sentence:

He was cut off out of the land of the living (Isa. liii. 8) was impossible for the prophet's contemporaries to comprehend fully, for the words contained a truth which could only be properly understood in the light of fuller revelation; but the evangelists must have realised how true they were, when they recorded: *There they crucified him* (Matt. xxvii. 35; Mark xv. 25; Luke xxiii. 33; John xix. 18). It would not be difficult to show how that almost the whole of this wonderful chapter is a prophecy concerning "The Son of Man" as the *Man of Sorrows.* This is acknowledged on all hands, so that it will not be necessary to emphasise it further. The reason, however, for which attention is drawn to this fact now is that our Lord Himself accepts the prophecy as applying to Him; quite apart from its fulfilment in His life and work, which we can see for ourselves, is *His* acceptation of it; this is clear, apart from many other quotations that could be given, from His words: *Behoved it not the Christ to suffer these things?* For it goes on to say: *And beginning from Moses and from all the prophets, he interpreted to them in all the Scriptures the things concerning himself* (Luke xxiv. 27). This means, therefore, that as regards that aspect of His teaching about the Son of Man which depicts Him as humiliated and despised He acknowledges the truth, the absolute truth, of what had been foretold. Is this not an *a priori* argument in favour of the fact that the prophecy concerning the *other* aspect of the Son of Man is also true? Let us enumerate the points in their logical sequence. The title "The Son of Man" in the Gospels is only used by our Lord; His teaching concerning "The Son of Man" consists of two parts which are apparently contradictory, and may be described by the two words: Humiliation, Glory. There are prophecies concerning each; in the former case the prophecy is seen to have been literally fulfilled in the life, suffering, and death of "The Son of Man"; but apart from this Christ corroborates the truth of what was prophesied, and confesses that it applied to Him. That is to say, the first part of His teaching concerning "The Son of Man" was proved to be true both in prophecy and fulfilment. The conclusion, therefore, is a fair one when it is contended that this fact justifies the presumption that the second part of the teaching is true also. It is not possible to separate the two elements in the teaching concerning "The

Son of Man," which our Lord so frequently emphasises; and, therefore, if one element has been historically proved to have been correct, there is an *a priori* probability that the second also will in the future be shown to have been correct.

It will have been noticed that the argument used is what might be termed "forensic," and is not one that would necessarily be asked for by believers with an unquestioning faith; but our sympathy has, so far, been with the large and growing numbers of those who find it very difficult to accept the New Testament teaching concerning the Second Advent; and the argument used, if carefully considered, must at least show the *precariousness* of declining to accept our Lord's words about His Second Coming. In our Law Courts the testimony of even the humblest witness is enhanced in value if he is known to have borne true testimony before. How much more, therefore, must this be so when Jesus Christ bears witness concerning Himself. It may, of course, be objected that much of what we read in the Eschatology of the Gospels does not belong to the original teaching of Christ, but has been put into His mouth by the compilers of the sources from which the Gospels were written; but a study of the eschatological passages in the Gospels and the teaching of our Lord on the subject shows that they constitute such a large portion of the whole material of the synoptic accounts that to regard them *in toto* as unoriginal, and therefore to deny their authenticity, is quite out of the question. Even were it granted that in some particulars words have been put into the mouth of Christ which He never uttered, this would not be of much use from the objector's point of view; *for the fact is that the Gospels are saturated with eschatological teaching.* Nor could we well expect it to be otherwise, for while it is undoubtedly true that Christ's teaching is full of guidance for life on this earth, yet the main importance of this life, according to that teaching, lies in the fact that it is merely preparatory for the world to come. The point of view of all the Gospel teaching is other-worldly, everything looks to the world to come, everything is subordinated to the thought of the Hereafter. How, then, should it be possible to eliminate the eschatological teaching of Christ, or any considerable part of it, from the Gospels? Is it always sufficiently realised how many of the parables are eschatological in character? It is not too much to say that the facts of the case compel us to see that the eschatological teaching in the Gospels is, in the main, Christ's; if it were not so the Gospels might as well never have been written.

§ii. But there is another consideration; a deeper one, and more difficult to follow; and neither believers nor doubters can afford to ignore it.

We know—or at all events we claim to know, owing to the fuller revelation that we have received from God—that Absolute Truth and the Godhead are inseparable. Our Lord, when standing before Pilate, said: *Every one that is of the truth heareth my voice*;[1] and to Pilate's answer: *What is Truth?* no reply was returned; He who had said: *I am the Truth* was standing before Pilate. Absolute Truth and the Godhead are inseparable. For this reason we find that some of the most cherished truths of Christianity are already adumbrated prior to the time of Christ; and if the Godhead and Truth must be in evidence at all times, it is what must be demanded when we find Truth irrepressible. Unquestionably it is the fact, that Truth will often be clothed in

[1] John xviii. 37, 38.

fantastic garb; but that is due to human fancy, not to anything that is wanting in Truth itself. If God is eternal, and if Truth is eternal, those things that are true must from their nature manifest themselves according to man's capacity for grasping the Truth. For this reason man's belief in a Creator, with all that that word implies for us, is inherent in Human Nature: also, man's yearning for a Redeemer is inherent in Human Nature. These facts are indisputable, as the study of the beliefs of primitive man prove.[1] If now—and this is the point that we have been aiming for—we find certain fundamental truths of Christianity in existence before the time of Christ, we have every justification for believing that since they belong to Truth, they belong also to *the nature of things*. Let an instance be given: The Incarnation generally, and in particular the Virgin Birth. Here is an instance of Virgin Birth—a pre-Christian instance: "It is said that one day the Virgin Ocrisia, a slave-woman of Queen Tanaquil, was offering, as usual, cakes and libations on the royal hearth, when a flame shot out towards her from the fire. Taking

[1] See the writer's *Religion a Permanent Need of Human Nature*, passim.

this for a sign that her handmaiden was to be the mother of a more than mortal son, the wise Queen Tanaquil bade the girl array herself as a bride and lie down beside the hearth. Her orders were obeyed: Ocrisia conceived by the god or spirit of the fire, and in due time brought forth Tullus Servius, the future King of Rome, who was thus born a slave, being the reputed son of a slave mother and a divine father, the fire god."[1] The *clothing* of the truth is folly; but that does not detract from the fact of the conception of the possibility of Virgin Birth being a true conception.

The belief in human gods, and divine men, is so universal among all races of the world, whether civilised or uncivilised, that it is unnecessary to give any examples;[2] but the existence of such beliefs shows that the conception of Incarnation lies in the nature of things.

In view of such things as these the alternative, of course, is as to whether Christianity has merely adapted heathen beliefs, or whether, as we have been trying to point out, Absolute Truth *must* assert itself, and that therefore

[1] Frazer, *The Early History of the Kingship*, pp. 218-219 (1905).
[2] Frazer, *The Golden Bough*, I., 137ff. (2nd Ed.).

these pre-Christian examples are merely adumbrations of truths which men in those times were incapable of understanding in their essential, spiritual meaning.

For Christians to whom the Truth has been revealed there can scarcely be any doubt about the matter. If there is anything in the Incarnation and the Virgin Birth which partakes of the nature of Absolute Truth, then they belong to *the nature of things*, a high, mysterious, super-sensuous "nature," but still belonging to the things that are. And therefore men have formed conceptions based upon these truths, just in the same way in which they formed their conceptions concerning the existence of God; that which is in the nature of things will and *must* find expression in one form or another in all ages, though the expression and form will necessarily vary according to man's varying capacity for apprehending Truth.

And now, after this necessary digression, to return once more, and quite briefly, to our main subject. Upon the analogy of what has just been said, we must regard, at all events in its essence, the pre-Christian teaching of the Second Advent as containing elements of Absolute Truth; for if we are justified, as we believe we are, in worshipping Jesus Christ as the Son of God, and in regarding His teaching as expressing in its essence Absolute Truth, then we must see in His words regarding the Second Advent not merely an adaptation of earlier teaching, but rather *the reiteration of Truth.* Or, to put it still more plainly, we set ourselves the question: What is one to say in view of the incontrovertible fact that a pre-Christian book has, in many vital particulars, the identical teaching on the Second Coming of Christ as that of the Gospels? The reply is that, inasmuch as that which partakes of the nature of Absolute Truth *must* assert itself—though it may be in very diverse garb—therefore in some form or another it will appear and press itself to the fore, at different periods of the world's history; so, as the teaching of the Second Coming, or, shall we say, of the Final Appearance on earth of The Son of Man, is in its essence Truth, therefore, in common with other truths, it pressed itself into the minds of receptive seers and became part of the world's common stock of accumulated Truth. At what particular time in the world's history men became cognisant of this particular item of Absolute Truth is really immaterial, since it must always have been in existence; but it received for us the final seal when Christ proclaimed that it *was* true.

Of course, it may be that we are entirely wrong; it may be that the whole pre-Christian teaching about this Second Coming is nothing more than speculative dreaming; it may be that words have been put into the mouth of Christ which He never uttered; or it may be, as some maintain nowadays, that Christ was mistaken in common with earlier Jewish teachers. All these things *may* be; but the point here insisted upon is that this great subject, in which so much is involved, cannot be dismissed off-hand in such a manner; there are too many elements that demand consideration in connection with it; it contains too much that is confessedly true, its intrinsic probability (as will be seen in a moment) is too great, than that it should be cast aside as incredible, at any rate by men who have the scientific sense. For what in its deepest signification is the *raison d'être* of the Second Coming? It is this: The final overthrow of Evil, and the Supremacy of Spirit; would anybody in their senses be prepared to deny that, at least, the best part of Humanity yearns for these things? Why, this, in the last instance, is the burden of every philosophical system that has ever been evolved; it is the goal of all things; it is that which every man and woman who has ever thought sufficiently about the subject is convinced must sooner or later come to pass. Who would acquiesce in the eternal existence of the principle of Evil? Who does not see that the spirit is greater than that which is merely material? Who would not welcome the final supremacy of spirit? What Christian does not *expect* this?

And this is what *in its essence* the Second Coming means; it must assuredly be apparent that this partakes of the nature of Absolute Truth. Or should objection be taken to the details which we read of in the accounts of the Second Coming? Enmities among men, plagues, wars, cataclysms and other cosmic disturbances? Alas, we know too well that most of these things are always prevalent among men, and if the *virus* of iniquity should work with more concentrated force on the eve of its final annihilation, there would really be nothing insurmountably incredible in that. As to the cosmic disturbances, it is still possible to see a moral significance in them. Nor need the language regarding the presence of angelic hosts, and the *rôle* assigned to them, be looked upon as entirely figurative. The moon being turned to blood, and the stars dropping from heaven, etc.—these elements are, likely enough, Oriental imagery; but *they* are not the things that trouble men's belief regarding the Second Coming. We must look to the larger issues, the permanent principles that are involved, the abiding element of Absolute Truth which the teaching concerning the Second Coming contains.

If this is done, then, it is maintained, that although we cannot in the nature of things *prove* the truth of Christ's teaching on the subject, nevertheless, as we have tried to show, the intrinsic probability of its truth makes it precarious to disbelieve in the doctrine of the Second Advent.

In so far as there has been Christian adaptation of Jewish teaching in this matter, it has been because the latter contained elements of Absolute Truth. *Think not that I came to destroy the Law, or the Prophets: I came not to destroy, but to fulfil.*

INDEX OF SUBJECTS

[*Roman figures denote chapters*]

www.ingramcontent.com/pod-product-compliance
Lightning Source LLC
LaVergne TN
LVHW050621100826
845148LV00011B/1680

* 9 7 8 1 5 9 2 4 4 5 9 6 7 *